DRUNK DRIVING

James Haley, *Book Editor*

Daniel Leone, *President*
Bonnie Szumski, *Publisher*
Scott Barbour, *Managing Editor*

An Opposing Viewpoints® Series

Greenhaven Press, Inc.
San Diego, California

Library of Congress Cataloging-in-Publication Data

Drunk driving / James Haley, book editor.
        p. cm. — (At issue)
    Includes bibliographical references and index.
    ISBN 0-7377-0796-8 (pbk. : alk. paper) —
ISBN 0-7377-0797-6 (lib. : alk. paper)
    1. Drunk driving—United States—Prevention. I. Haley, James, 1968– . II. At issue (San Diego, Calif.)

HE5620.D72 D78   2002
363.12'514—dc21   2001050146

Contents

Introduction

On the night of May 14, 1988, Larry Mahoney was drunk, so drunk that his blood-alcohol concentration—the percentage of alcohol in his blood—was more than twice Kentucky's legal limit at the time of .10 percent. Regardless, Mahoney got behind the wheel of his pickup truck and proceeded to drive northbound in the southbound lane of Interstate 71 near Carrollton, Kentucky, crashing head-on into a church bus returning from an amusement park. The collision ruptured the bus's gas tank, causing a fire that killed twenty-three children and four adults and injured a dozen others, mostly as a result of smoke inhalation. Mahoney had no recollection that he had caused the deaths of twenty-seven people until he woke up in a hospital bed the following morning with minor injuries. He was subsequently convicted of assault, manslaughter, wanton endangerment, and drunken driving and was sent to the Kentucky State Reformatory, where he served a nine-and-a-half-year sentence.

Many observers believe Mahoney deserved a more severe sentence for his crime. This fact is a testament to how much the public's attitude toward drunk driving has changed since the late 1970s, when it was not perceived as criminal behavior. This sea change in public perception was what Candy Lightner set out to accomplish when she founded Mothers Against Drunk Driving (MADD) in 1980. Lightner's thirteen-year-old daughter, Cari, was killed by a drunk hit-and-run driver as she walked down a suburban street in California. The driver, who had been convicted four times of driving while intoxicated (DWI) prior to taking Cari's life, received a two-year prison sentence, but was permitted to serve time in a work camp and a halfway house. Outraged by the leniency of the sentence, Lightner focused MADD on raising public awareness of drinking and driving as a serious crime and advocated tough legislation to deter and apprehend drunk drivers.

Beginning in the early 1980s, the lobbying efforts of MADD began to have a significant influence on federal and state policy to combat drunk driving. Based on statistics showing that sixteen- to twenty-year-olds, although only 10 percent of the nation's licensed drivers, were involved in 20 percent of all fatal alcohol-related crashes, then-president Ronald Reagan signed into law the National Minimum Drinking Age Act on July 17, 1984. The law mandated that states raise their minimum drinking age to twenty-one or lose federal highway funds. By the mid-1990s, all fifty states had complied. States also instituted tougher penalties for drunk drivers, such as mandatory jail terms for first-time offenders and on-the-spot driver's license suspensions for those failing or refusing to take a breath test. Data from the Department of Transportation show overall alcohol-related fatalities declining 36 percent between 1982 and 1997.

In the 1990s, prevention advocates focused on changing federal law to lower the level at which drivers are presumed to be legally intoxicated based on their blood-alcohol concentration (BAC). Primarily determined by breath tests administered by police officers during traffic stops, BACs indicate the level of impairment drivers may be experiencing due to the percentage of alcohol in their blood. Until the late 1990s, most states enforced a .10 percent BAC. To reach this level of intoxication, the average 170-pound man would have to consume slightly more than five twelve-ounce beers in an hour. That same man would reach the lower .08 percent BAC limit favored by prevention advocates after consuming four twelve-ounce beers in an hour. On October 23, 2000, then-president Bill Clinton signed into law a national .08 BAC standard as part of the Transportation Appropriations Bill. States that do not lower their BAC limit to .08 by 2004 will lose 2 percent of their federal highway money. As of summer 2001, twenty-six states had set their BAC limits at .08.

According to the Insurance Information Institute, 16,068 people were killed in 2000 in alcohol-related motor vehicle crashes, a 1.8 percent increase over 1999, and alcohol continues to be a factor in 38 percent of all traffic fatalities. Proponents of .08 BAC laws believe that these statistics demonstrate the need for stronger deterrence and prevention measures to continue the progress being made against drunk driving. MADD contends that the level of intoxication permitted by states with .10 BAC laws allows for dangerously impaired driving, and that adopting the .08 BAC limit in every state will save over 500 lives each year. Explains MADD, "The vast majority of drivers, even experienced drinkers, are significantly impaired at .08 with regard to critical driving tasks such as braking, steering, changing lanes, divided attention tasks, and judgement. . . . If every state adopted a .08 BAC . . . law, hundreds of lives would be saved every year, with thousands of injuries prevented and millions of dollars saved."

An April 1999 study of all fifty states conducted by the National Highway Traffic Safety Administration (NHTSA) confirmed MADD's assertions. It compared states with .08 BAC laws to states with .10 BAC laws before and after the laws were passed. The study found that states that passed .08 BAC laws reduced the involvement of drunk drivers in fatalities by 8 percent. It also estimated that 274 lives had been saved in states that had passed .08 BAC laws and that if all fifty states enacted .08 BAC laws, 590 lives could be saved each year.

Supporters of .08 BAC also value the deterrent effect the laws have on potential drinking drivers who might otherwise choose to drive themselves home under the more lenient .10 BAC limit. The editors of Drivers.com, a website providing information on driver safety and behavior, argue that .08 BAC laws send the message to drivers that even though they might not feel drunk after a few drinks, their driving ability is substantially impaired. "Alcohol impaired drivers at .08 BAC, who crash at a much higher rate than drivers who have not taken alcohol, . . . typically do not *feel* impaired. . . . A problem with setting legal BAC near limits at which impairment becomes visible [such as .10 BAC] is that it tends to send a wrong message to drivers that there is no impairment at lower levels, a few drinks becomes OK." The tendency of .08 BAC laws to make those who have consumed alcohol more aware of their impaired driving ability, combined with the message that states are cracking down on drunk driving, will deter more drunks from getting behind the wheel, according to .08 BAC proponents.

Opponents to a national .08 BAC standard contend that drivers are not dangerously impaired after reaching .08 BAC and that the overwhelming majority of alcohol-related fatalities are caused by drivers with BAC levels much higher than .08. Supporters of this view, ranging from trade associations for the alcohol, bar, and restaurant industries to individuals concerned with protecting civil liberties, assert that instead of preventing drunk driving fatalities, .08 BAC laws result in the arrest of responsible social drinkers. Argues Eric Peters, a nationally syndicated automotive columnist, "Studies . . . have found that most alcohol-related crashes involve motorists with BAC levels of 0.12 or higher. These 'super drunk' motorists are the ones doing the damage—yet the social drinker is taking most of the flack. The majority of drivers arrested for 'driving under the influence' . . . were not driving erratically or giving any evidence of impairment." By wasting time arresting harmless motorists, police enforcement of .08 BAC does little to solve the problem of chronic drunk drivers with high BACs. MADD's founder Candy Lightner, who left the organization in the mid-1980s and went to work as a lobbyist against .08 BAC laws for the American Beverage Institute in 1994, agrees with Peters. She has said that "police ought to be concentrating their resources on arresting drunk drivers—not those drivers who happen to have been drinking. I worry that the movement I helped create has lost direction."

Civil libertarians are troubled by the fact that .08 BAC laws establish an arbitrary level at which a driver is presumed to be drunk—particularly since that level is one that many people reach after consuming two or three drinks. These critics point out that many factors affect a person's reaction to alcohol, including their weight, metabolism, and how much they have had to eat. In addition, driver impairment is not solely caused by the consumption of alcohol. Explains Jim Holt, a philosophy and public policy writer for the *Wall Street Journal,* "Drivers talking on cell phones . . . have the same accident rate as drivers with a blood alcohol level of 0.10%. . . . Elderly drivers are more deadly still. . . . Clearly there are many 'impaired' drivers on the road who present a far greater peril than do drivers with a blood alcohol level between 0.08% and 0.10%." For these reasons, drivers with .08 BACs should be punished only if they cause an actual accident or commit traffic violations like speeding or running a red light, according to Holt.

Because the consequences of driving while legally intoxicated involve tough penalties such as mandatory jail terms, heavy fines, license suspensions, and even the confiscation of motor vehicles in some jurisdictions, the issue of a nationwide .08 BAC standard has serious implications for drivers. Convinced that a .08 BAC law in every state will send a message to the American public that drunk driving is a criminal act that simply will not be tolerated, groups like MADD are continuing to pressure state lawmakers to get in line and adopt the federal .08 BAC standard. Other observers are not at all convinced that punishing responsible drinkers with criminal convictions is a just solution to a problem primarily caused by chronic drunk drivers. Under the threat of losing federal highway funds, it seems inevitable that all fifty states will eventually enact .08 BAC laws. Given this victory, prevention groups may begin to push for even lower BAC limits in the next decade, a battle that should certainly become heated.

Enormous gains have been made against drunk driving over the past twenty years and have created the general impression that drunk driving is largely under control. The contentious debate over .08 BAC laws demonstrates, however, that not all motorists are comfortable with the loss of personal freedom and invasion of privacy that increasingly accompany prevention measures. Reformers run the risk of losing the public's support if their efforts to eliminate drunk driving appear too punitive toward responsible drinkers. Whether or not .08 BAC laws are a fair and effective solution to the problem of drunk driving is one of the issues discussed in *At Issue: Drunk Driving*. The authors also discuss the problem of chronic drunk drivers, underage drinking, the use of sobriety checkpoints and passive alcohol sensors, and confiscating the cars of convicted drunk drivers.

1

Lower Blood-Alcohol Concentration Limits for Drivers Will Save Lives

National Highway Traffic Safety Administration

The National Highway Traffic Safety Administration (NHTSA), a division of the U.S. Department of Transportation, conducts safety programs to reduce deaths, injuries, and economic losses resulting from motor vehicle crashes.

The blood-alcohol concentration (BAC) is the measurement used to determine the amount of alcohol present in a person's body. Drivers with blood-alcohol concentrations of .08 percent and above experience significant impairment of their driving abilities, increasing their risk of being killed or injured in motor vehicle crashes. Twenty-six states have lowered BAC limits to .08 percent from .10 percent or higher, enabling the conviction of seriously impaired drivers. However, opposition to new .08 laws continues due to pressure from the alcohol and hospitality industries. Because the American public strongly supports legislation and programs to deter drunk driving, .08 BAC laws will gain supporters as more people come to understand how BACs are determined and how many lives could be saved with a .08 limit in every state.

[Editor's note: In October 2000, Congress passed the national .08 percent blood-alcohol concentration (BAC) standard as part of the Transportation Appropriations Bill. States that do not adopt .08 BAC laws by 2004 will lose 2 percent of their federal highway money.]

The amount of alcohol in a person's body is measured by the weight of the alcohol in a certain volume of blood. This is called the blood alcohol concentration, or "BAC." Because the volume of blood varies with the size of a person, BAC establishes an objective measure to determine levels of impairment.

Reprinted from *Setting Limits, Saving Lives: The Case for .08 BAC Laws*, a publication of the National Highway Traffic Safety Administration (Washington, DC: U.S. Government Printing Office, 1999).

The measurement is based on grams per deciliter (g/dl), and in most states a person is considered legally intoxicated if his or her BAC is .10 g/dl or greater; that is, alcohol makes up one-tenth of one percent of the person's blood.

A driver's BAC can be measured by testing the blood, breath, urine or saliva. Breath testing is the primary method used by law enforcement agencies. Preliminary breath testing can be performed easily during a roadside stop using a hand-held device carried by police officers. It is non-invasive and can even be performed while the person is still in his or her vehicle.

Evidentiary breath testing equipment is evaluated for precision and accuracy by the National Highway Traffic Safety Administration (NHTSA). Test instruments approved by NHTSA as conforming to specifications are accurate within plus or minus .005 of the true BAC value.

State BAC levels

All states but two (Massachusetts and South Carolina) have established BAC *per se* levels. Seventeen of those states plus the District of Columbia have set that level at .08 (Alabama, California, Florida, Hawaii, Idaho, Illinois, Kansas, Maine, New Hampshire, New Mexico, North Carolina, Oregon, Texas, Utah, Virginia, Vermont and Washington). . . . [Since this viewpoint was written, nine more states have set their BAC level at .08. They are: Arizona, Arkansas, Georgia, Indiana, Iowa, Kentucky, Maryland, New York, and Rhode Island.]

With each drink consumed, a person's blood alcohol concentration increases. Although the outward appearances vary, virtually all drivers are substantially impaired at .08 BAC. Laboratory and on-road research shows that the vast majority of drivers, even experienced drivers, are significantly impaired at .08 with regard to critical driving tasks such as braking, steering, lane changing, judgment and divided attention. In a recent study of 168 drivers, every one was significantly impaired with regard to at least one measure of driving performance at .08 BAC. The majority of drivers (60–94%) were impaired at .08 BAC in any one given measure. This is regardless of age, gender, or driving experience (see chart, "BAC and Impairment").

Although the outward appearances vary, virtually all drivers are substantially impaired at .08 BAC.

The risk of being in a motor vehicle crash also increases as the BAC level rises. The risk of being in a crash rises gradually with each BAC level, but then rises very rapidly after a driver reaches or exceeds .08 BAC compared to drivers with no alcohol in their system.

A recent study found that the risk of being killed in a single vehicle crash at .08 to .099 BAC ranged from 11 times the risk at .00 BAC for older drivers to 52 times the risk at .00 BAC for young male drivers.

Setting the BAC limit at .08 is a reasonable response to the problem of impaired driving. This is not a couple of beers after work or a glass or

Blood Alcohol Concentration (BAC) and Areas of Impairment

	BAC	
	.10	
	.09	
	.08	concentrated attention, speed control
	.07	
information processing, judgment	**.06**	
	.05	
	.04	concentration
eye movement control, standing	**.03**	
	.02	tracking and steering
steadiness, emergency responses	**.01**	divided attention, choice reaction time, visual function

two of wine with dinner. At .08, everyone is impaired to the point that driving skills are degraded. Most states that have lowered their BAC to .08 have found a measurable drop in impaired driving crashes and fatalities, as have many countries that have adopted .08. . . . [The lower limit] also serves to deter driving after drinking. Crash statistics show that even heavy drinkers, who account for a high percentage of driving while intoxicated (DWI) arrests, are less likely to drink and drive because of the general deterrent effect of .08. At the same time, lowering the BAC limit to .08 makes it possible to convict seriously impaired drivers whose BAC levels are now considered marginal because they are at or just over .10.

.08 laws work

The effect of California's .08 law was analyzed by NHTSA, which found that 81% of the driving population knew that the BAC limit was stricter (from a tremendously successful public education effort). The state experienced a 12% reduction in alcohol-related fatalities, although some of this can be credited to the new administrative license revocation (ALR) law. The state also experienced an increase in driving under the influence (DUI) arrests.

The second multi-state analysis of the effect of lowering BAC levels to .08 was conducted by Ralph Hingson, Sc.D., a professor at Boston University's School of Public Health and Chairman of the school's Social and Behavioral Sciences Department, along with two other researchers. The results of their study were reported in the September 1996 issue of the *American Journal of Public Health,* a peer-reviewed journal.

Hingson compared the first five states to lower their BAC limit to .08 (California, Maine, Oregon, Utah and Vermont) with five nearby states that retained the .10 limit. Overall, the .08 states experienced a 16% reduction in the proportion of fatal crashes with a fatally injured driver whose BAC was .08 or higher, as well as an 18% reduction in such crashes with a fatally injured driver whose BAC was .15 or higher.

The immediate significance of these findings is that, not only did the .08 BAC laws reduce the overall incidence of alcohol fatalities, but also reduced fatalities at the higher BAC levels. The effect on extremely impaired drivers (the "problem drinking drivers") was even greater than the overall affect.

The study concluded that if all states lowered their BAC limits to .08, alcohol-related highway deaths would decrease by 500–600 per year.

In a NHTSA analysis of these five states (Johnson and Fell, 1995), significant reductions in alcohol-related fatal crashes were found in four out of the five states ranging from 4% to 40% when compared to the rest of the states with .10 BAC laws.

Impaired driving affects us all

About two out of every five Americans will be involved in an alcohol-related crash at some time in their lives, and many of them will be innocent victims. There is no such thing as a drunk driving accident. Virtually all crashes involving alcohol could have been avoided if the impaired person were sober.

As BAC levels rise, so does the risk of being involved in a fatal crash. Recent research has shown that, in single vehicle crashes, the relative fatality risk for drivers with BACs between .08 and .099 is at least 11 times greater than for drivers with a BAC of zero and is 52 times greater for young males.

In the United States, BAC limits are set by states. The limit of .10 found in [many] states is the highest in the industrialized world.

An eleven state study also examined the effects of .08 BAC (and ALR) laws. It found that .08 BAC legislation was associated with reductions in alcohol-related fatalities, alone or in conjunction with ALR laws, in seven of the eleven states studied. In five of these states (VT, KS, NC, FL, NM), implementation of the .08 BAC law itself was associated with significantly lower rates of alcohol-related fatalities. These results take into account any pre-existing downward trends the states were already experiencing, due to other factors such as the presence of other laws, use of sobriety checkpoints, etc. In two states (CA and VA), significant reductions were associated with the combination of .08 BAC and ALR laws, implemented within six months of each other. This study also found evidence of reduced alcohol (beer) consumption in several states following implementation of .08 laws.

The third study analyzed the effects of a .08 BAC law implemented in 1993 in North Carolina, a state which had already been experiencing a sharp decline in alcohol-related fatalities since 1987. This study concluded that there was little clear effect of the lower BAC limit. Results from various analyses suggested that some portion of the reductions may have been associated with the law but the magnitude of these effects was not sufficient to make this conclusion.

In aggregate, these three recent studies provide additional support for the premise that .08 BAC laws help to reduce alcohol-related fatalities, particularly when they are implemented in conjunction with other impaired driving laws and programs. Nearly all of the findings of these and previous studies show changes that suggest that .08 BAC legislation (as well as .10 BAC laws and ALR laws) have contributed to the trend toward reduced alcohol-related crashes and fatalities that have been experienced across the nation.

NHTSA, the federal agency charged with the safety of motor vehicles and our nation's highway safety, has long supported .08 state laws. In a 1992 Report to Congress, the agency recommended that all states lower their illegal *per se* limit to .08 for all drivers 21 years and above. (NHTSA supports zero tolerance for drivers under the legal drinking age. Numerous other federal agencies with an interest in public health and safety issues, as well as dozens of private sector organizations, support NHTSA's call for universal .08 state laws.

As a public policy to deter impaired driving, .08 has lagged behind other countermeasures such as *per se*, administrative license revocation and zero tolerance for those under 21. Nearly all states have *per se*, the vast majority have ALR and all have zero tolerance.

But the passage of new .08 laws have been few and far between, despite consistent evidence that they work, because some organizations in the alcohol and hospitality industries oppose any and all such proposals at the state level. This is both sad and ironic, since these industries have not only been strong supporters of many other anti-impaired driving laws, but have also been crucial partners in getting safety messages out to hard-to-reach audiences.

Promotions such as designated driver programs and sober ride/call-a-cab efforts showcase their concern, generate enormous goodwill from the general public and raise awareness. It is tragic that some of the same companies and trade associations that have launched excellent server training programs, public information campaigns and other efforts to reduce impaired driving so vigorously oppose legislation when it comes to .08.

As BAC levels rise, so does the risk of being involved in a fatal crash.

A report by the General Accounting Office (GAO), which reviewed the currently available .08 BAC studies stated that, while the evidence of impact of .08 BAC laws is not conclusive, "there are . . . strong indications that .08 BAC laws, in combination with other drunk driving laws (particularly license revocation laws), sustained public education and information efforts, and vigorous and consistent enforcement, can save lives."

We commend GAO for reaching the sound and accurate conclusion that a .08 blood alcohol concentration (.08 BAC) law can be an important component of a state's overall highway safety program. We agree that highway safety research shows that the best countermeasure against drunk driving is a combination of laws, including .08 BAC, sustained public education, and vigorous enforcement and we agree that there are strong indications the .08 BAC laws, when added to existing laws and programs, are associated with reductions in alcohol-related fatalities.

With regard to whether the studies are "conclusive," it must be pointed out that all research is equivocal and therefore, by that definition, inconclusive. In context, however, particularly with the addition of the recently released studies conducted by NHTSA, the evidence is consistent and convincing that, in most states where .08 BAC laws have been added to existing impaired driver control efforts, they have been associated with reductions in alcohol-related fatalities.

Recent research by NHTSA and past studies by the Boston University School of Public Health and the California Department of Motor Vehicles have shown impaired driving reductions already attributable to .08, as well as the potential for saving additional lives if all states adopted .08 BAC laws. Not only would deaths and injuries go down, but costs would as well. Alcohol-related crashes cost society $45 billion every year, not including pain, suffering and lost quality of life.

Myths about .08 BAC

Myths about .08 abound, many proliferated by those who actively oppose .08 laws. Here are a few of the commonly heard myths, countered by research-based facts from the National Highway Traffic Safety Administration, academic and scientific institutions, and credible private sector organizations such as Mothers Against Drunk Driving.

MYTH: "If you lower the BAC limit to .08, it means I can't even have a couple of drinks with my dinner."

FACT: While there is no "safe" amount of alcohol for drivers, most people can drink moderately and drive legally when the illegal *per se* limit is set at .08. A 170-pound male typically would have to consume more than four drinks in one hour on an empty stomach to reach a BAC of .08. A 135-pound female typically would have to consume three drinks in the same time frame.

MYTH: "I know when I'm 'too drunk to drive' —I don't need to be concerned about my blood alcohol concentration."

FACT: Your driving skills can be seriously compromised even when your behavior is not observably "drunk." Alcohol causes impairment in reaction time, attention, tracking, comprehension and other skills essential for safe driving. Even when attempting to drive carefully, an impaired driver cannot compensate for those reduced abilities. In addition, alcohol affects your ability to judge whether or not you are impaired.

MYTH: "The American public does not support .08 because most people have no idea how much alcohol it would take to put them over the legal limit."

FACT: According to several national surveys, most Americans would not drive after having two or three drinks in one hour, an amount that would put them below .08. Most people know how much alcohol it takes to impair their driving ability and they accept lower limits such as .08 for adults.

MYTH: ".08 BAC legislation will not affect problem drinker drivers who have high BAC levels."

FACT: The latest research shows that .08 laws not only reduce the incidence of impaired driving at lower BACs, they also reduce the incidence of impaired driving at high BACs over .10 (Voas and Tippetts, 1999). A .08 law serves as a general deterrent to drinking and driving, sends a message that the state is getting tougher on impaired driving, and makes people think twice about getting behind the wheel after they've had too much to drink. .08 is a key part of a complete package to reduce impaired driving. While problem drinker drivers do account for a significant part of the DWI problem, most fatally injured drinking drivers (70–80%) had no prior alcohol-related offenses. A comprehensive anti-impaired driving program must use all available laws and programs to reduce DWI.

MYTH: "Lowering the BAC limit to .08 places an unnecessary strain on the law enforcement community by forcing officers to monitor the behavior of currently legal drivers and pay less attention to the real problem, repeat offenders and those with high BACs."

FACT: Lowering the *per se* limit to .08 does not place an unnecessary strain on police. Officers still must have probable cause to stop and test drivers to determine if they are impaired. A .08 law will actually make it easier for police to arrest drivers at .10 or .11 BACs because these are no longer "borderline" cases.

MYTH: "If you start arresting people driving with a .08 BAC, you will clog up the court system."

FACT: In the largest state, California, the .08 law has had little impact on the state's judicial system. No increases have been reported in the proportion of arrested drivers who plead guilty, request jury trials or appeal convictions. .08 is a deterrent to impaired driving, especially when coupled with other effective anti-DWI measures. Anything that reduces the incidence of DWI reduces the overall burden on society, including the judicial system.

Recent research by NHTSA and past studies . . . have shown . . . the potential for saving additional lives if all states adopted .08 BAC laws.

MYTH: ".08 is just the first step toward even lower BACs and eventually another attempt at prohibition."

FACT: Widely accepted public health research has identified .05 as the BAC level at which driving skills begin to deteriorate. Because of this, some organizations—most notably the American Medical Association—officially support .05 as the safest limit. However, safety professionals generally do not believe such laws would have any reasonable chance politically in this country. Even those organizations that have adopted such policies accept .08 as the best reasonable and acceptable compromise that will save lives, prevent injuries and reduce costs to society. The notion that safety organizations seek a return to prohibition is unfounded.

MYTH: "The United States General Accounting Office (GAO) says .08 BAC laws do not work."

FACT: The GAO report actually stated the following: "Overall, the evidence does not conclusively establish that .08 BAC laws, by themselves, result in reductions in the number or severity of alcohol-related crashes."

They went on to say: "There are, however, strong indications that .08 BAC laws in combination with other drunk driving laws (particularly licence revocation laws), sustained public education and information efforts, and vigorous and consistent enforcement can save lives." Of course, .08 BAC laws do not save lives by "themselves." They must be publicized as enforced and work in combination with the other laws of the state. The evidence shows that, in aggregate, when states adopt .08 BAC laws, they can save lives, especially in combination with administrative licence revocation laws which 40 states already have.

Polls support anti-DWI efforts

The American public overwhelmingly supports legislation and programs to curb impaired driving. In a poll conducted for Mothers Against Drunk Driving (MADD), the Gallup Organization found that the vast majority of the American public considers drunk driving the number one major highway safety problem and most support tough laws and sanctions to reduce impaired driving.

All of the approaches to deal with impaired driving do well in public opinion polls, but the programs that have received more attention in the media and other public forums—ALR, zero tolerance, sobriety checkpoints and vehicle confiscation for repeat offenders—poll higher than .08. The likely reason is that people do not understand the technical aspects of how BACs are determined and what .08 means in real terms. When it comes to their own tolerance for alcohol and their own abilities, however, the American public is certain: most say they would not drive after consuming two or three drinks in one hour.

The challenge for .08 supporters is to help people make a connection between their own common sense and the public policy that would define impaired driving as .08. Clearly, the more people know about the problem and the potential solutions, the more they support changes to bring about those solutions. .08 is a key part of any public health initiative that aims to reduce society's burden from impaired driving.

Supporters of .08 have many allies and resources to call upon, both at the national level and in the states.

Federal and State Governments and several private sector organizations hold workshops, publish idea samplers and planners, and offer other helpful organizing tools that may help .08 supporters achieve their public policy goals.

One of the arguments used against .08 is the impact on the law enforcement and judicial system. However, when the largest state, California, lowered the BAC limit to .08, there was little impact on court administrators or judges.

The main impact in California has been on prosecutors' decisions concerning whether or not cases should be filed. Previously, those arrested for DWI with BACs below .12 typically were allowed to plea to reduced charges. Since the limit was changed, this plea-bargain "cut off" has dropped to about .10 BAC. No increases were reported in the proportion of DWI defendants pleading guilty, requesting jury trials, or appealing convictions.

Modern breath analysis equipment is easy to use during a roadside stop, whether the legal limit is .08 or any other limit. The devices are small enough and inexpensive enough that every patrol car on traffic duty can be equipped with one. Law enforcement officers can administer the test quickly and easily, without the driver even leaving the car. If the preliminary breath test shows the person is not impaired, motorists can be on their way and police can continue their duties. .08 does not change the fact that law enforcement officers can conduct these roadside tests quickly and easily.

.08 is supported by law enforcement organizations, including two of the largest: the International Association of Chiefs of Police and the National Sheriffs' Association. These organizations and others like them would not support a law that is unenforceable, ineffective or burdensome on police officers.

Treatment can help

Medical treatment programs for repeat offenders—and sometimes even first time offenders—have become an increasingly popular part of the sentencing process. Some states require certain treatments while others recommend but do not require them.

This leads to concern that programs will be overcrowded with long waiting lists. Most safety organizations recommend that impaired driving programs be self-supporting. Fines and fees paid by offenders should cover the cost of all sentencing, including treatment for alcoholism or alcohol abuse. This reduces the burden on taxpayers while helping to ensure that offenders get the help they need.

Medical treatment for impaired drivers, whether required by law or ordered at the discretion of a judge, correctly positions impaired driving as a public health problem. .08 laws do not contribute to burdens on society but help to identify those with a problem and get them into programs to reduce the chance they will eventually kill or injure themselves or someone else.

> *.08 is a key part of any public health initiative that aims to reduce society's burden from impaired driving.*

.08 is a reasonable BAC level. A .08 BAC is not reached with a couple of beers after work or a glass or two of wine with dinner. The public supports .08, and surveys show that most people would not drive after consuming two or three drinks.

As a public health initiative and a traffic safety policy, .08 works and works well, especially in combination with other laws and programs. A .08 BAC *per se* law will:

- Increase the arrest and conviction rates for impaired drivers at .10 and above;
- Raise the perceived risk of arrest for driving after drinking;
- Improve public awareness about how much alcohol it takes to be dangerously impaired; and

• Bring the U.S. closer to *per se* limits of most industrialized nations.

If every state adopted a .08 *per se* law, hundreds of lives could be saved every year, with thousands of injuries prevented and millions of dollars saved. But even more important would be all the extra birthday candles that would get blown out, the graduation ceremonies that would be attended, the weddings that would be celebrated and the millions of everyday smiles that would be exchanged.

No one will ever know if they or one of their loved ones will be the next victim of impaired driving, just as no one will ever know if they are the one who was spared thanks to good public policy. .08 is sensible, reasonable and effective. It's time to adopt .08 in every state.

Bibliography

"The Impact of Lowering the Illegal BAC Limit to .08 in Five States in the U.S.," by Delmas Johnson and James Fell, National Highway Traffic Safety Administration, Washington, DC, 39th Annual Proceedings of the Association for the Advancement of Automotive Medicine, Chicago, IL, October 16–18, 1995.

"The Relationship of Alcohol Safety Laws to Drinking Drivers in Fatal Crashes," by Robert B. Voas and A. Scott Tippetts, Pacific Institute for Research and Evaluation, Bethesda, MD, for the National Highway Traffic Safety Administration, April, 1999.

2

Lower Blood-Alcohol Concentration Limits for Drivers Will Not Save Lives

American Beverage Institute

The American Beverage Institute (ABI) is an association of restaurant operators that serve alcohol. The institute conducts research to educate policymakers about the laws and issues surrounding the sale of beer, wine, and spirits.

Pressuring states to lower their arrest thresholds for drunk driving to a .08 percent blood-alcohol concentration (BAC) punishes responsible social drinkers, whose level of impairment poses less of a risk than talking on a cell phone while driving. Close to two-thirds of all alcohol-related fatalities involve drivers with BACs of .14 percent and above, and lowering the legal BAC limit will have no effect on the behavior of chronic drunk drivers who consistently flaunt current laws. Prevention efforts are better spent aggressively targeting the small percentage of alcohol abusers responsible for the majority of alcohol-related accidents with on-the-spot driver's license suspensions and tougher punishment.

After a decade and a half of resounding success in the war against drunk driving, we have come to a crossroads.

The relentless campaign against drunk driving has succeeded in stigmatizing this reckless crime, reducing the issue to what some have described as an alcoholism problem. Responsible social drinkers have changed their behavior to avoid driving drunk at all costs. Alcohol abusers continue to get drunk and climb behind the wheel.

Avoiding an ineffective strategy

As a result, the overwhelming successes we have come to expect have been transformed to a gradual decline in drunk driving deaths. *The New York Times* has reported that "the people heeding the message are not the

Reprinted from "The .08 Debate: What's the Harm?" American Beverage Institute, Washington, D.C. Reprinted with permission.

ones who drink the most," and it may be time for "some states and judges to try new strategies."[1]

Unfortunately, the leading strategy . . . [supported by Congressional legislation] and several state legislatures is to lower the arrest threshold for drunk driving to a .08% blood-alcohol concentration (BAC). This strategy punishes behavior that is not a part of the drunk driving problem. Nothing has divided the once-united front against driving while intoxicated (DWI) more than this issue. [Editor's note: In October 2000, Congress passed the national .08 percent blood-alcohol concentration (BAC) standard as part of the Transportation Appropriations Bill. States that do not adopt .08 BAC laws by 2004 will lose 2 percent of their federal highway money. As of summer 2001, twenty-six states had complied.]

To better understand the facts surrounding the complicated and sometimes heated .08% BAC debate, the American Beverage Institute prepared this viewpoint to answer three vital questions: What is .08% BAC? Does it work? What *does* work in the fight against drunk driving?

.08% BAC and the law

According to the National Highway Traffic Safety Administration (NHTSA), a 120-pound woman with average metabolism will reach the .08% BAC threshold if she drinks two six-ounce glasses of wine over a two-hour period.[2] This woman is hardly what most people think of as a dangerous drunk driver. Yet under the proposed .08% legislation, she would face arrest, fines, mandatory jail, loss of license and insurance rate increases of 200–300%.

Meanwhile, the real problem of alcohol abusers who drive goes unabated. According to the U.S. Department of Transportation (U.S. DOT), the average BAC level among fatally injured drinking drivers is .17%, more than twice the proposed .08% arrest level. Nearly two-thirds of all alcohol-related fatalities involve drivers with BACs of .14% and above.[3] Lowering the legal BAC limit will have no effect on drivers who already ignore the current law.

Getting to a .17% BAC is no easy task. An average-sized man would have to drink 10 beers in two hours—or a beer every 12 minutes—to get to that level. And remember, that's just the *average* BAC level among fatally injured drinking drivers.

Some advocates of the .08% legislation proclaim that the average-sized man must have four or five drinks in an hour to reach a .08% BAC. In reality, few people drink four or five drinks in one hour, and then voluntarily quit. They are at .08% for a moment but keep drinking and generally do not become .08% *drivers*. This "4–5 drinks in an hour" mathematical possibility is an example designed to enrage rather than enlighten. This pattern of a drink every 12 to 15 minutes is typical of product abusers who drink to BAC levels well above .08% over several hours before driving.

By diluting the definition of "drunk driver" to include social drinkers, lawmakers will automatically increase the pool of "drunks" by more than 50% without increasing the resources to fight it. This will have a debilitating effect on the already under-funded law enforcement efforts to stop truly drunk drivers.[4]

Alcohol-related vs. alcohol-caused

A single-vehicle accident occurring late at night involving absolutely no alcohol can be—*and often is*—classified as an "alcohol-related" accident, according to the U.S. DOT.

The same is true for fatal accidents in which alcohol is present but not the cause of the accident. By the government's definition, if a sober driver barrels through a red light and kills a woman driving responsibly after drinking a glass of wine, that is an alcohol-*related* accident. Ditto if the sober driver kills a jaywalker who has had as little as one drink.[5]

Most fatal accidents involving BAC levels below .10% are alcohol-*related*, not alcohol-*caused*. Almost all fatal accidents involving BAC levels of .17%—the average BAC level among fatally injured drinking drivers—are alcohol-*caused*. Let's go after the cause of drunk driving fatalities—the alcohol abuser who drives.

Projected impairments vs. actual experience

Proponents of lowering the drunk driving arrest level like to *project* fatality rates based upon driver impairment. Depending upon whom you ask, alcohol-related fatality rates *are projected to increase* 10 to 16 fold at the .08% BAC level due to driver impairment. Strangely, no NHTSA accident data support these claims.

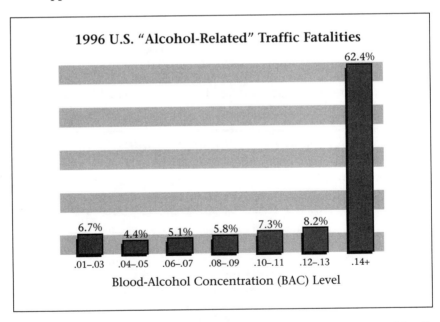

1996 U.S. "Alcohol-Related" Traffic Fatalities

BAC Level	Percentage
.01–.03	6.7%
.04–.05	4.4%
.06–.07	5.1%
.08–.09	5.8%
.10–.11	7.3%
.12–.13	8.2%
.14+	62.4%

Blood-Alcohol Concentration (BAC) Level

In fact, according to 15 years of NHTSA data, the percentage of fatalities involving .08% drivers is virtually the same as the percentage involving drivers with BACs of .03%, .02%, even .01%. And even the most ardent anti-alcohol zealot doesn't believe that these low BAC alcohol-*related* accidents are alcohol-*caused*.[6]

Why the contradiction? Simple. Responsible social drinkers self-regulate regardless of BAC levels. When people feel that it's best to hand the keys to someone else, they do.

There's a lesson here: When sorting out such a serious public policy issue, it's better to look back at the facts than try to *predict* the future.

According to a study in the *New England Journal of Medicine*, the risk of getting into a car accident while talking on a cellular phone is the same as driving with a .10% BAC—the current "drunk driving" threshold in most states.[7]

The effort to lower the drunk driving threshold to .08% BAC would have drivers arrested, jailed and suffer fines, loss of license and higher insurance rates for behavior that is less risky than talking on a cellular phone while driving.

No credible research

There is not one piece of credible evidence that proves .08% BAC legislation saves lives. Although the U.S. DOT has funded numerous studies in the 15 years since the first .08% BAC law went into effect, the agency has been unable to demonstrate that .08% BAC laws save lives.

When [former] U.S. DOT Secretary Rodney Slater endorsed the *federal* proposal to lower the arrest level to .08% BAC, he did not cite any government research to bolster his case. Instead, he cited a discredited three-page report written by Ralph Hingson, a sociologist with a well-known anti-alcohol bias.

It should come as no surprise that Sec. Slater was reluctant to refer to NHTSA's own .08% research. In 1995, the NHTSA conducted a study of the first five states that went to .08% BAC by looking at the impact in six categories. Of these 30 "measures," NHTSA found decreases in nine of them. The 21 other measures showed the alcohol-related fatality rate *actually increased* or failed to move.[8]

[Lowering] the arrest threshold for drunk driving to a .08% blood-alcohol concentration (BAC) . . . punishes behavior that is not a part of the drunk driving problem.

Statistically, reductions in DWI linked to .08% were not proven.

Further, the authors of the report admitted their analysis "does not account for other potentially important factors, e.g., other alcohol legislation, that could influence the impact of the .08 BAC legislation." In other words, even the nine decreases are suspect.

According to Dr. William Latham of the University of Delaware in an analysis of the NHTSA report, "These results cast serious doubt on the validity of the contention that simply lowering the BAC limit from .10% to .08% will significantly reduce fatalities."[9]

Lower-BAC proponents claim a 1991 government study proved that California's alcohol-related fatality rate went down 12% after that state adopted .08%.[10]

National Highway Traffic Safety Administration, U.S. Department of Transportation (August 1991).

11. "The General Deterrent Impact of California's .08% Blood Alcohol Concentration Limit and Administrative Per Se License Suspension Laws," Research and Development Section, Division of Program and Policy Administration, California Department of Motor Vehicles (September 1995).

12. R. Hingson, T. Heeren and M. Winter, "Lowering State Legal Blood Alcohol Limits to 0.08%: The Effects on Fatal Motor Vehicle Crashes," *American Journal of Public Health*, vol. 86, no. 9 (September 1996).

13. Robert A. Scopatz, Ph.D., "Analysis of 1975–1993 Fatal Crash Experience in States with .08% Legal Blood Alcohol Levels," (Washington, D.C.: American Beverage Institute, May 1997).

14. National Highway Traffic Safety Administration "State Legislative Fact Sheet," (Washington, D.C.: U.S. Department of Transportation, October 1996).

15. National Highway Traffic Safety Administration, "1996 Drivers of vehicles in transport with known alcohol-test results," *Fatal Accident Reporting System* [CD-ROM and database on-line] (Washington, D.C.: U.S. Department of Transportation, 1996).

16. "Status Report on Alcohol-Related Traffic Crashes in the United States for 1995." *The Century Council Report* (Los Angeles: 1995).

17. Hans Laurel, "Effects of Lower BAC Limits in Sweden," Swedish National Road Administration. Presented at the Annual Transportation Research Board Conference, Session 390, Sheraton Washington Hotel, Wednesday, January 14, 1998.

18. National Highway Traffic Safety Administration "1996 Drivers of vehicles in transport with known alcohol-test results," *Fatal Accident Reporting System* [CD-ROM and database on-line] (Washington, D.C.: U.S. Department of Transportation, 1996).

3

Preventing Underage Drinking Will Reduce Drunk Driving Fatalities

Elizabeth Shepard

Elizabeth Shepard is a freelance journalist and author of the novel H.

Underage drinking is an enormous problem among America's youth, leading to tragic consequences for teenagers who are regularly injured or killed in drunk driving accidents. To combat media messages that portray alcohol as sexy and fun, and to reduce the ease with which many teenagers can purchase alcohol, parents must join forces with federal and state governments in communicating to children the dangers associated with alcohol use. Such efforts should include stronger alcohol education, improved treatment for abusers, and better enforcement of the minimum drinking age. These steps are necessary to reduce the staggering human and monetary costs of underage drinking.

Eighteen-year-old Leah Bean gave up alcohol in 1998. During her junior year in high school, Leah's best friend, April, was killed in a crash after leaving a party where kids had been drinking. The 19-year-old driver with whom April was riding crashed the car while driving with a blood alcohol content of .20 percent—more than twice the legal adult limit in Tennessee. According to Leah, the teens knew that party-goers were drinking and that the store which sold the teens alcohol was notorious for not checking IDs. But Leah echoes other teens' feelings of invincibility, admitting it is "as if there's a bubble around 15- to 21-year-olds that prevents bad things from happening."

Leah represents thousands of teenagers whose lives have been devastated by underage drinking. According to Monitoring the Future, a survey conducted by the University of Michigan, 31 percent of 12th-graders reported binge drinking (five or more drinks in a row) in the two weeks prior to the survey. Fifty-one percent reported consuming alcohol. Of eighth-graders, 15 percent reported binge drinking—and 24 percent consumed alcohol.

Many parents allow their teenage children to drink alcohol at home in an effort to teach them how to drink responsibly. They may have good intentions, but the results can be deadly. What they do, in fact, is facilitate their kids' comfort with alcohol, and the trouble only begins there. . . .

"Kids don't know where to draw the line," Leah explained. "When parents open the door to alcohol for their kids, their kids figure if it's OK to drink at home, it's OK to drink out, too."

Many parents would be shocked to learn how young their children are when they begin to drink. Youth tend to begin drinking alcohol when they're as young as 12 years old. A new study shows a four-in-one chance that kids who begin drinking at 13 will become problem drinkers—and most likely impaired drivers—as opposed to young people who don't drink until the age of 21. By the time teenagers get to college, their rate of consumption has escalated dramatically: 4.4 million of them are binge drinkers and another 1.8 million are heavy drinkers (consuming five or more drinks on one occasion at least five times in the past month).

In some cases, parents aren't even aware that the underage and excessive drinking is taking place. A good example is spring break. Many parents send their kids off on trips to relax and play in the sun. Most often, these vacations are weeklong drinking junkets or "booze cruises" with excessive alcohol consumption.

At the other extreme, parents sometimes acknowledge the drinking and help their teens plan parties hoping to ensure their safety by "controlling" their drinking environment. This was the case for teens from Highland Park, a wealthy Dallas suburb. Police broke up a warehouse party in Dallas and found that parents had rented the facility and contracted a bus company to safely deliver drunken high school students to and from the party.

Setting clear boundaries

But no matter how challenging parents may feel it is to communicate with their kids about alcohol, talking to them and setting clear boundaries are the most important things they can do. Survey after survey shows that young people rank parents among the top reasons for not using alcohol, demonstrating that parents have a great deal of impact and influence on their child's decision on whether to drink.

Laws holding parents liable for underage drinking incidents are becoming more common. It is evident that young people alone are not at the root of the underage drinking issue—adults often facilitate youth drinking by providing or buying the drinks.

Alcohol is everywhere

In 1998, about 10.4 million drinkers in the United States were less than 21 years old. Sure, it's illegal, but that doesn't mean kids can't get their hands on alcohol.

In fact, 75 percent of young teens say that alcohol is easy to acquire. Approximately two-thirds of teenagers who drink report that they buy their own alcohol. Whether they buy it from stores or at bars that sell without carding, from home delivery services improperly monitored by state laws or from friends and siblings, alcohol is everywhere and easily within youths' reach.

The Lawrence County, Tennessee, MADD Youth In Action team conducted a study to see how many merchants sold alcohol to minors. Young men and women who were at least 21 years old but looked younger were sent into stores to try to purchase alcohol. The results were shocking: 48 percent of all salespeople never asked to see the buyers' identification. Of those sellers who asked, 50 percent of them sold the alcohol even after the buyers said they had no ID.

Adults often facilitate youth drinking by providing or buying the drinks.

And it seems that underage drinkers make alcohol a priority in their budgets. Each year, college students spend approximately $5.5 billion on alcohol—more than they spend on soft drinks, milk, tea, coffee and books combined.

One 19-year-old college student, who wished to remain anonymous, said, "The drinking starts on Thursday nights and continues throughout the weekend. When one party runs out of alcohol, we all move on to another party. We drink until we can't drink another shot. Kids keep count of how many drinks they have each night; it's like a contest. When my parents send me my monthly check for living expenses, I make sure I save enough money to buy beer."

A dangerous "free-for-all"

Teresa Robinson's 21-year-old daughter, Nicole, a college student, was killed in an alcohol-related crash November 13, 1997. "A group of kids went to a bar near campus to celebrate someone's 21st birthday, and they proceeded to get extremely drunk. Everyone at the bar knew that the kids were underage and drunk; but no one stopped them. The bartenders just kept serving everyone more drinks. I was stunned that no one in the bar tried to prevent the kids from getting in their cars."

Nicole was intoxicated when she got into the car being driven by a girl who was so drunk she fell on her face at the bar in front of the bartenders. The driver, with a blood alcohol content of .24 percent, was driving nearly 100 miles per hour when she crashed into a tree. The driver lived. Nicole died at the scene of the crash.

Teresa and her husband had cautioned Nicole never to drink and drive, and they never consumed any alcohol in front of their kids. "We were very conscientious about teaching our children about the dangers of alcohol. But I don't know how to get kids to listen. The media glorifies alcohol. The commercials are enticing. When kids get to college, it's a free-for-all—no one's watching them or saying yes or no. Kids who attended Nicole's funeral still drink and party and drive!"

Even parents who set good examples and have discussed the rules regarding alcohol use have a tough battle. Advertisers—which spend more than $1 billion each year on alcohol advertisements alone—still portray alcohol as alluring and exciting for youth.

Whether via an advertisement or through careful product placement, images of alcohol in the media have become ubiquitous. A recent study funded by the Office of National Drug Control Policy (ONDCP) examined top-rated television network series broadcast between October and December 1998.

The results: alcohol was consumed in 71 percent of all episodes, including 65 percent of the programs most popular with teenagers. About one-third of all the episodes were set in bars, nightclubs or restaurants where alcohol was consumed. 40 percent of the episodes made drinking look like a positive experience, while only 10 percent portrayed alcohol use negatively. Only 1 percent of the episodes portraying alcohol usage showed a refusal to use alcohol.

The nationwide cost of its most menacing drug

With happy hours, discounts on wine coolers and nickel-beer nights at bars near colleges, alcohol may be society's least expensive drug, but it is one of its most costly. Underage drinking costs the United States more than $58 billion every year—enough to buy every public school student a state-of-the-art computer.

Couple that with 1998 figures which calculate that alcohol-related traffic crashes cost this country $18,242,000,000 and you begin to see the devastating losses. But society pays a larger price than a monetary one. The death rate associated with youth alcohol use is staggering. Alcohol kills 6.5 times more youth than all other illicit drugs combined. The three leading causes of death for 15- to 24-year-olds are automobile crashes, homicides and suicides—alcohol is a leading factor in all three.

It would make sense, then, for the government to initiate and commit to a full-force effort to eradicate youth alcohol use. Surprisingly, when the federal government launched a five-year, $1 billion youth anti-drug media campaign, alcohol was excluded.

The power of the drug alcohol

Alcohol itself and the powerful nature of its effects on young bodies is also a mighty force in America's No. 1 youth drug problem.

To put it simply, the effects of alcohol are seductive, potent and hazardous. Alcohol has absolutely no beneficial effects on teenagers, and its use needs to be taken seriously for what it is—perilous.

"Alcohol interacts with many different systems," explained Scott Swartzwelder, Ph.D., clinical professor at Duke University and author of *Buzzed: The Straight Dope About the Most Used and Abused Drugs from Alcohol to Ecstasy* (W.W. Norton, 1998). "It causes sedative effects and relieves anxiety, among other things. In teens, there is less of a sedative effect and that is dangerous and misleading for teens."

"The brain systems that give drinkers positive feelings may adapt to the alcohol and come to need it," Dr. Swartzwelder continued. "After repeated use, the brain systems come to feel that something is missing when alcohol is denied, and this motivates people to drink even more. Eventually, people drink to prevent the negative effects they feel from not drinking."

The adolescent brain is particularly susceptible to the powerful effects of the drug alcohol. "We know that alcohol consumption can impact learning and memory in the adolescent brain," Dr. Swartzwelder said. "The dangers and long-term consequences of alcohol use among teens are not fully understood."

A silent enemy and a deafening need for treatment

"Alcohol is the silent enemy," said Suzanne Smith, director of planning for operations at Phoenix House in Texas, the nation's leading substance abuse treatment, prevention and education organization. "Underage drinking remains a consistent problem. Society makes it accessible, and since it's legal for adults, the rules are confusing for adolescents. They don't really understand that alcohol is harmful to them."

In addition, alcohol is "the gateway drug" insofar as it's the precursor to teenagers trying many other types of substances. "Just about every kid who's being treated for drug abuse is mixing their drug of choice—be it marijuana or heroin or something else—with alcohol," said Smith.

According to Smith, "Most adolescents don't seek treatment on their own, and a parent, caretaker or more often than not the criminal justice system guides them to the help they need. Unfortunately, there are few long-term treatment programs available that provide teens with the structure they need to effect lasting changes in their behaviors, attitudes and values. As a result, only 10 percent of those who need help actually get it," so the problem can spiral out of control.

But treatment can work, and teenagers can be taught how to re-claim their lives by learning how bad alcohol really is for their bodies and for their future. "Treatment is really the second line of defense," Smith added. "Parents are unquestionably their children's first and most important teachers. They need to have heart-to-heart talks with their kids and give them accurate information about consequences of abusing alcohol and other substances."

Treatment is a win-win proposition: helping kids deal with their addiction and lead sober lives paves the way for them to become constructive, contributing citizens. And for every dollar society spends in treating addicted teens, it saves $12 on the criminal justice, health care and welfare systems.

First steps for alcohol-free youth

Greg Hamilton has been the chief of law enforcement of the Texas Alcohol Beverage Commission (TABC) for nearly seven years, and he said he's beginning to see a change nationwide.

"People in communities across the country are starting to get on board with this issue, but it takes time," he said.

"The TABC attacks the problem of underage drinking with a two-pronged approach: enforcement and education," he said. "We want to elicit voluntary compliance with the law by holding parents, kids, store owners and other adults responsible for giving or selling alcohol to minors. We take action against them and issue citations. We hold them accountable for their actions, and we educate them about the underage-drinking problem."

The TABC also educates law enforcement agents about the issue. "Law enforcement, like any other agency, is short staffed," Hamilton noted. "They used to tend to see underage drinking as a low priority, thinking that 'kids would be kids' and go through a drinking phase. But lately, police, store owners and parents are beginning to take the issue more seriously and doing something about it."

Advertisers—which spend more than $1 billion each year on alcohol advertisements alone—still portray alcohol as alluring and exciting for youth.

Still, more can be done. "Parents need to send a clear message that kids are not allowed to drink, and stop providing alcohol to their kids," he said. "High schools and colleges need to hold kids accountable for their actions when they buy or consume alcohol. And faith groups need to talk about the problem and educate the community."

Facing reality

We can no longer point fingers at "bad kids" or negligent parents. Society as a whole bears the burden of the tragic consequences of underage drinking. MADD says that efforts to tackle the problem must involve parents—who, in their best efforts, can sometimes make uninformed and dangerous decisions. Retailers and the law enforcement community must strengthen their resolve to uphold the existing laws designed to protect young people. The media must be diligent in responsibly and accurately portraying the dangers of alcohol use by teens. Advertisers must cease targeting young people in marketing alcohol and alcohol-related products. Those who produce television shows and movies must take responsibility for the underage-drinking images they portray. Communities nationwide must provide treatment centers to help young people work their way back to alcohol-free lives. We must partner with youth.

Youth have emerged as a major force in the efforts to tackle underage drinking. All across the nation, young people are banding together to put an end to America's No. 1 youth drug problem. They not only are taking action, they are making a difference.

By linking arm-in-arm with these young people, we can eradicate the nation's most devastating youth drug problem—alcohol.

4

Zero Tolerance Laws Deter Underage Drinking and Driving

Office of Juvenile Justice and Delinquency Prevention

The Office of Juvenile Justice and Delinquency Prevention (OJJDP) develops prevention and intervention programs in response to juvenile delinquency and victimization.

In response to the large of number of deaths of fifteen- to twenty-year-olds resulting from alcohol-related motor vehicle crashes, all fifty states have enacted zero tolerance laws which make it illegal for drivers under the age of twenty-one to operate a vehicle while they have a blood-alcohol concentration (BAC) greater than .02 percent. In most states, the penalty for violating this law is suspension or revocation of the driver's license. The deterrent effect of zero tolerance laws has led to a significant reduction in alcohol-related vehicle crashes and fatalities for drivers ages fifteen to twenty.

D rinking alcohol before driving is extremely risky behavior for young people who lack experience and judgment. Over 33 percent of all deaths of 15- to 20-year-olds result from motor vehicle crashes, and in 1996, the alcohol-involvement rate for young drivers was approximately double the rate for the over-21 licensed driver population (NHTSA, 1997). This phenomenon may be due to the fact that young drivers have less experience with both drinking and driving. They also may lack the fundamental skills needed to assess realistically the hazards posed by various driving situations.

All states (plus the District of Columbia) have enacted a law to prohibit underage drivers from operating a motor vehicle after drinking. The details of the laws, such as the precise permissible blood alcohol concentration (BAC), vary from state to state. Zero tolerance laws, when properly implemented and enforced, can be effective in sending a no-use message to young people and preventing alcohol-related crashes among young

Excerpted from "Zero Tolerance," in *A Guide to Zero Tolerance and Graduated Licensing: Two Strategies That Work*, prepared for the Office of Juvenile Justice and Deliquency Prevention by the Pacific Institute for Research and Evaluation, 1998.

drivers. This viewpoint presents a brief overview of the strategy and reasons for the nearly nationwide spread of zero tolerance laws. It explains the importance of publicity and enforcement of such laws and discusses challenges that can accompany low BAC enforcement.

What is zero tolerance?

Zero tolerance laws prohibit young persons from driving a vehicle while they have a BAC greater than 0.00 percent, 0.01 percent, or 0.02 percent. If a police officer has probable cause to believe that a driver has been drinking, the officer administers a breath test. In most states with zero tolerance laws, any amount of alcohol in the body of a driver under 21 is an offense for which the driver's license may be suspended for a period of time (NHTSA, 1996). Because of the high value young drivers place on their licenses, the threat of license revocation has proven to be an especially effective sanction—for both its punitive and its deterrent effect—for this age group (NHTSA, 1996).

The most commonly specified BAC for drivers under 21 is 0.02 percent, which is approximately equal to one drink for the average person (36 states). Twelve states and the District of Columbia have adopted the 0.00 percent level and two states, 0.01 percent (NHTSA, 1998).

The first four states to reduce the legal BAC limit for young drivers were Maine (July 1983), North Carolina (September 1983),Wisconsin (July 1984), and New Mexico (July 1984). These states experienced a 34 percent decline in nighttime fatal crashes among adolescents targeted by the lower BAC levels. This decline was approximately one-third greater than a similar decline observed in four selected nearby comparison states (Hingson, Heeren, & Winter, 1991).

By the end of 1990, 12 states had lowered BAC levels for youth. These 12 experienced a 16 percent decline overall in nighttime single-vehicle fatal crashes among young drivers targeted by the new laws, compared with a 1 percent rise among drivers of the same age in selected comparison states. Of the 12 states, four had adopted a BAC level of 0.00 percent, four had a level of 0.02 percent, and 4 had levels ranging from 0.04 percent to 0.06 percent. Measured crash reductions were statistically significant for the 0.00 percent states (22 percent reduction) and the 0.02 percent states (17 percent) but not for the 0.04 percent to 0.06 percent states (7 percent). It was estimated that if all states adopted a 0.00 percent or 0.02 percent level for drivers ages 15 to 20, at least 375 nighttime single-vehicle fatal crashes would be prevented each year (Hingson et al., 1994).

Appropriate penalties for zero tolerance violations

All states have laws against driving while intoxicated (DWI) or operating a motor vehicle while under the influence of alcohol. These laws carry severe penalties, including a possible jail sentence, loss of license, and a substantial fine. A second or third impaired-driving arrest can lead to a felony conviction. Under zero tolerance laws, lesser charges are typically brought against young drivers; the strategy is not intended to send young persons to jail or to produce a criminal record.

The penalties for a violation vary widely across the states, but they nearly always involve the suspension or revocation of the driver's license. In some states, the term of the license suspension can be equal to or greater than the term of suspension for a DWI conviction. They may also involve alcohol or drug assessment, some form of alcohol or drug education or treatment, and a fine. High fines, jail, house arrest, the creation of a felony conviction record, and vehicle impoundment—all possible consequences of a DWI conviction—are not part of sanctioning for zero tolerance.

Generating public awareness

A public awareness campaign can dramatically increase the effectiveness of the law. Maryland experienced an 11 percent statewide reduction in the number of drivers under age 21 who had been drinking and crashed following the implementation of its 0.02 percent zero tolerance law. However, in six counties where a special public education campaign was implemented, alcohol-related crashes among young drivers were reduced by 50 percent (Blomberg, 1993). The campaign included television and radio commercials that featured local police officials as spokespersons. A pamphlet and matching poster with the theme "You don't have to be drunk to lose your license in Maryland" also were distributed to support the broadcast campaign. As with most other types of traffic enforcement, effects are greatest when the law and efforts to enforce the law are well publicized.

When considering enforcement issues, it is essential to keep in mind that detecting, apprehending, and punishing violators is not as important as deterring young people from drinking and driving in the first place. Deterrence is strongest when people believe that their punishment will be swift and severe. Therefore, well-publicized enforcement campaigns in which the apprehended offenders receive penalties are extremely important—even if there are many offenders who are not caught.

Zero tolerance laws . . . can be effective in . . . preventing alcohol-related crashes among young drivers.

Zero tolerance laws require somewhat different enforcement strategies from those used for traditional impaired driving patrols. Police officers are often reluctant to stop young people. Officers need to be trained to take enforcement action when identifying low levels of alcohol in young drivers. Such training might include knowledge of the statute, application of implied consent under the statute, and procedures for handling juveniles. In general, officers identify these violations only after the vehicle has been stopped for some other reason such as speeding or suspected DWI over the 0.10 percent or 0.08 percent adult legal limit. Unlike for DWI, there are currently no standardized, documented cues to aid officers in the detection of zero tolerance violators within a moving traffic stream.

One tool that may eventually prove helpful in zero tolerance enforcement is the passive alcohol sensor. Such devices test the air around a driver for possible traces of alcohol from exhaled breath. They do not require the driver's active cooperation. Such devices have proven to be quite effective at sobriety checkpoints in identifying drivers at or near the legal limit (see Ferguson et al., 1995). However, the currently available passive devices were designed for enforcing the adult drinking driver statutes, and hence, higher legal adult alcohol limits. While they may prove useful for enforcing zero tolerance at checkpoints, these sensors appear to be less well suited for the enforcement of very low levels of alcohol during regular patrols (Leaf & Preusser, 1996).

In six [Maryland] counties where a special [zero tolerance] public education campaign was implemented, alcohol-related crashes among young drivers were reduced by 50 percent.

It should also be noted that enforcement of any laws that involve juveniles can be difficult. In most states, juvenile offenders cannot be incarcerated with adults and, once arrested, may not be released except to a parent, guardian, officer of the court, or special juvenile facility. This may cause an officer to be kept off patrol for a long period while the arrest is processed and the parents are located. Communities that want their police to conduct this type of enforcement need to provide support personnel and facilities where the identified juvenile violators, typically those under the age of 18, can be handled.

Sending a "no-use" message to young people

Elevated crash risk among teenage drivers can be seen after only one or two drinks. The goal of zero tolerance is to eliminate driving by young persons who have consumed any alcohol. Beginning with Maine in 1983, zero tolerance laws have now been adopted by most States. Substantial crash reductions have been documented, particularly in those places where the law has been well publicized. Further, zero tolerance laws provide consistent no-use messages to young people. Challenges that remain include finding more effective strategies for zero tolerance enforcement and related publicity.

References

Blomberg, R.D. (1993). Lower BAC limits for youth: Evaluation of the Maryland .02 law. In *Alcohol and other drugs: Their role in transportation* (Transportation Research Circular No. 413, pp. 25–27). Washington, DC: National Research Council, Transportation Research Board.

Ferguson, S.A.,Wells, J.K., and Lund, A.K. (1995). The role of passive alcohol sensors in detecting alcohol-impaired drivers at sobriety checkpoints. *Alcohol, Drugs & Driving*, 11, 23–30.

Hingson, R., Heeren, T., and Winter, M. (1991). Reduced BAC limits for young people (impact of night fatal crashes). *Alcohol Drugs and Driving*, 7, 117–27.

Hingson, R., Heeren, T., and Winter, M. (1994). Lower legal blood alcohol limits for young drivers. *Public Health Reports*, 109, 738–44.

Leaf, W.A., and Preusser, D.F. (1996). *Effectiveness of passive alcohol sensors*

(DOT HS 808 381). Washington, DC: National Highway Traffic Safety Administration.

National Highway Traffic Safety Administration. (1996). *Zero tolerance laws to reduce alcohol-impaired driving by youth: State legislative fact sheet.* Washington, DC: U.S. Department of Transportation.

National Highway Traffic Safety Administration. (1997). *1996 Youth fatal crash and alcohol facts* (DOT HS 808 525). Washington, DC: U.S. Department of Transportation.

National Highway Traffic Safety Administration. (1998). *Traffic safety facts, 1997: Young drivers.* Washington, DC: Author.

5

A Legal Drinking Age of 21 Does Not Reduce Drunk Driving

Dan Levine

Dan Levine is a staff writer for the Hartford Advocate.

Intended to reduce the number of alcohol-related traffic fatalities, the minimum drinking age of twenty-one became the law in 1984 as then-President Reagan gave in to pressure from anti–drunk driving activists. There remains, however, no conclusive evidence that declines in traffic fatalities can be attributed directly to the passage of this law. Many factors, such as education, designated driver programs, and free taxi services from bars and restaurants have raised public awareness about the perils of drunk driving. In addition, the age twenty-one drinking law has unintended negative consequences. Many high school and college students rebel against this restriction on their freedom and consume alcohol in an irresponsible manner, resulting in reckless and violent behavior. To eliminate alcohol's enticement as a "forbidden fruit," the drinking age should be restored to eighteen, enabling young adults to learn how to drink responsibly in controlled social situations.

Prohibition will always occupy a place of great honor in the American pantheon of political idiocy.

Forgotten lessons of Prohibition

That spectacular experiment died in a torrent of Tommy gun shells that overwhelmed the temperance movement, which had worked so diligently for its passage. And the United States government, along with the rest of the country, learned a valuable lesson: regulating the social mores of a nation is almost impossible. If the people want something badly enough, they will find a way to get it.

Our government has already forgotten that lesson. By raising the le-

Excerpted from "Wasted: Why Our Drinking Laws Will Never Work," by Dan Levine, *Hartford Advocate*, August 24, 2000. Reprinted with permission from *Hartford Advocate*.

gal drinking age from 18 to 21 in the mid-1980s, President Ronald Reagan and Congress brought the federal government back into the alcohol prohibition business. Sure, the ban affected a smaller group of people, but it is a ban nonetheless.

Fourteen years after Prohibition became law in 1919, American political leaders recognized their mistake and took corrective action, repealing the ban. Now, 14 years have passed since every state was forced into a 21-year-old purchase limit.

It is time to fix another mistake.

An ineffectual law

The traditional argument for restoring the drinking age to 18 years old is straightforward: 18-year-olds can vote and die for their country, so their throats should be able to feel the burn of Jack Daniels. If you can toss a grenade, you should certainly be able to toss back a shot of tequila.

That face value argument seems especially relevant given that current laws are completely ineffectual. Illegal boozing continues in large levels at universities across the country. Eighteen- to 20-year-old frat boys have few qualms about the law as they hook their mouths up to a beer bong and drink themselves to oblivion.

But a deeper and more powerful argument for why the current law will never work can be found in simple psychology. Some researchers believe that by banning alcohol among this age group, the government has actually made drinking more attractive. It's a fact of human nature. Just watch a toddler cry in a toy store when his parent says he can't have that B-B gun.

18-year-olds can vote and die for their country, so their throats should be able to feel the burn of Jack Daniels.

So denying something like alcohol always makes us want it more. The law seems even more inane given that college, with its protected setting and proximity to drinking establishments, is, in some ways, the perfect environment in which to learn to drink responsibly. That it remains an illegal drinking venue for most of its inhabitants seems an ill-conceived irony.

"By making [drinking] a 'don't,' we actually make it a 'do,'" says Dr. Morris Chafetz, who served as a member of Reagan's commission to study drunk driving.

Irresponsible drinking and "forbidden fruit"

"Although the legal purchase age is twenty-one years, a majority of college students under this age consume alcohol—certainly not a surprise to anyone," writes Ruth Engs, a professor of applied health sciences at Indiana University, in an article for *Vermont Quarterly*. "When they have the opportunity to drink, they do so in an irresponsible manner because drinking by these youth is seen as an enticing 'forbidden fruit,' a 'badge of rebellion against authority' and a symbol of 'adulthood.'"

Engs believes more irresponsible drinking has led to increased trouble with the law, along with more dire alcohol-related side effects. It is all part of a governmental policy that encourages young people to wallow in potentially destructive behavior.

Researchers who believe in the "forbidden fruit" lure of underage drinking trace their theoretical lineage back to University of Kansas psychology professor Jack Brehm.

Brehm published his theory of psychological "reactance" in 1966. Reactance is an intense motivational state that occurs when people believe their freedom is being unfairly restricted. Often people will react by trying to get around the restriction, possibly through rebellion.

A simple experiment proposed by West Virginia University professor Steve Booth-Butterfield illustrates the theory. A child plays with two toys and likes each one equally. The researcher places the toys a few feet apart. Then he puts a large piece of Plexiglas in front of one of the toys, so the child can see it but can't get to it. The child is asked to pick a toy.

"Of course, the child immediately toddles over to the toy with the Plexiglas barrier and starts wailing," says Booth-Butterfield. "He will plow into the glass like a little robot. He will pound on the plex. He will try to crawl over it like a Marine in boot camp. He will do everything but go after the other toy that is freely and easily available to him. He wants THAT one!"

More, not less, underage drinking

Marketing journals have published articles exploring reactance as a tool in advertising campaigns. Engs has been one of the leaders in applying the theory to underage drinking patterns. Engs conducted a study during the 1987–88 academic year to test whether the then new 21-year-old drinking age produced reactance among college students. She discovered that raising the minimum legal purchase age did not reduce underage drinking.

Instead, other researchers in academia found exactly the opposite. Lynn Zimmer, a sociology professor at Queens College, says she taught at a small college in upstate New York at the time.

"I watched a fascinating thing happen. There was always a lot of drinking associated with campus," she says, "but suddenly it seemed around Thursday everybody was talking about what they were going to drink that weekend, and making a plan (to make it happen)."

Chafetz, a professor at Harvard in the 1980s, agrees. He says he started hearing a common theme from his students, along the lines of: "Boy, I can't wait until the weekend to get bombed."

These researchers believe that raising the drinking age made getting wasted a sexier priority. It is a classic example of reactance.

Drinking to extremes

Advocates for keeping the drinking age at 21 often point to studies by the National Highway Traffic Safety Administration (NHTSA) that show a drop in underage drinking since 1986. For example, 91.3 percent of high school seniors said they had had a drink in 1986. That dropped to 80 percent by 1997, according to a University of Michigan study.

Proof positive for a 21-year-old limit? Not quite, say critics. Drinking patterns in all age groups, under and over 21 years, fell in the same time period. In 1986, the average American consumed 2.58 gallons of ethanol per year. That was down to 2.18 percent in 1997.

Even if the raw number of high school seniors has dropped, Engs's research demonstrated that those who do drink take it to an extreme. According to her study of violent behavior associated with drinking among college students, in 1991, 35 percent of heavy drinkers reported getting into a fight at least once in the previous 12 months after boozing.

That is up from 25.9 percent in 1982. And it plays directly into the reactance theory take on glorifying rebellious behavior.

But beyond reactance theory, Chafetz argues for basic respect for young adults. He also points out a basic contradiction with a ban on drinking in undergraduate school.

Undergraduate life is as much about becoming an independent person and making your own choices as it is about pure book learning. It carries an implicit message of freedom for the student, many of whom are away from home for the first time.

"When you have been dependent on your parents for your identity, college is about breaking loose," Chafetz says. "You want something to differentiate yourself. That's why a 'don't' is a 'do.'"

Prohibiting something like alcohol, then, while at the same time conveying a message of freedom, creates an explosive situation.

Europe's example

European countries are often cited as proof that lower drinking age limits do not lead to American-style binge drinking habits.

In the Netherlands, Professor Peter Cohen of the University of Amsterdam says Dutch students are not isolated on a particular campus. In the United States, university students "live in big dorms," which creates "big herds" of people that accentuate heavy drinking. In Amsterdam, students are more independent and do not fall into the same culture.

Holland is also known for its tolerant policies towards marijuana. In Holland, marijuana is bought and sold freely, and yet the Dutch use it less than Americans. The drug is prohibited by law in the United States, making it more attractive as an outlet of rebellion.

Raising the drinking age made getting wasted a sexier priority.

In light of those policies, Cohen has conducted research on marijuana use in the Netherlands and compared it to the United States. His findings are startling. Only 15.6 percent of Dutch people over 12 years old have ever used marijuana, while 32.9 percent of Americans have. Cohen is currently studying marijuana rates in Amsterdam and San Francisco, and he says the numbers are quite similar.

These numbers clearly lend credence to reactance theory. And since reactance kicks in when freedom is threatened, it must be exacerbated in

Americans. We are taught since birth to cherish our "freedom." But Cohen thinks his research highlights the irrelevance of drug and alcohol policies as a whole.

"I think alcohol policy is not very important. It is nothing more than an expression of a complex culture," he says.

Drinking goes "underground"

Researchers also argue that a higher drinking age reduces the opportunity for young adults to learn how to drink responsibly in social situations. As a professor at the University of Wisconsin, Alan Marlatt (now at the University of Washington) remembers when alcohol sales were permitted in the student union. If someone started trouble or passed out, a sober person was always on hand to take care of the situation.

By banning that kind of socialization, drinking has been forced underground, Zimmer says, with less supervision. Gone are the professor/student functions that serve wine, where students can learn to drink without getting blotto.

"The infantilization of young adults stands in the way of promoting safe drinking," says Ethan Nadelmann, founder and director of the Lindesmith Center-Drug Policy Foundation, the nation's leading organization advocating for drug policy reform in the U.S. and abroad.

Pressure to reduce fatalities

Examining that irresponsible behavior only becomes more important when the issue of safe driving, one of the main public relations arguments used to raise the drinking age to 21 in the 1980s, is examined.

Groups like Mothers Against Drunk Driving (MADD) began to bring more and more public attention to drunk driving fatalities in the early part of the 1980s. Grassroots pressure brought about Reagan's Presidential Commission on Drunk Driving, formed in 1982.

Chafetz served as chairman of the commission's Education and Prevention Committee. He says he was the lone voice in favor of keeping the drinking age at 18.

But he did not issue a minority report to go along with the commission's findings, handed to Reagan in December of 1983. That report recommended raising the drinking age to 21 in an attempt to curb drunk driving, Chafetz says.

On July 17, 1984, Reagan signed the National Minimum Drinking Age Act that affirmed each state's right to decide its own minimum purchase age.

Or at least they could in theory. To help ensure states chose the correct age limit—i.e., 21—Reagan made an offer they couldn't refuse.

According to the bill, states who didn't accept a 21-year-old limit would lose 10 percent of their share of federal highway dollars. That state would continue to lose 10 percent every year until it changed its laws.

In a masterstroke, Reagan blackmailed 32 states into accepting the 21-year-old limit. The law went into effect March 26, 1986, when the NHTSA, along with the Federal Highway Administration, made it part of their respective regulations.

Congressman Scott Klug (R-Wisconsin) introduced a bill that challenged the regulations on state's rights grounds in 1996. The bill died a quick death in committee.

21-year-old limit: a solution to drunk driving?

Advocates for a 21-year-old purchase limit continue to cite statistics on motor vehicle accidents and fatalities as their number one argument for the success of the law.

Indeed, the stats look compelling. According to the NHTSA, 50 percent of all fatalities in 1988 were alcohol-related. That fell to 38 percent ten years later. From 1988 until 1998, the NHTSA says drivers 16 to 20 years old experienced the largest decrease in intoxication rates in fatal crashes (33 percent).

In Connecticut, 59.9 percent of all motor vehicle fatalities were alcohol-related in 1985. That number dropped ten percentage points to 49.2 percent in 1996, according to the NHTSA.

Reform advocates . . . do not believe lower alcohol-related fatalities are directly linked with raising the drinking age.

Before 1986, young adults often fled 21-limit states and drove to places that had an 18-year-old age, according to Jeffrey Hon, spokesman for the National Council on Alcohol and Drug Dependence, an advocacy group that favors a 21-year-old limit. That is part of the reason for the drop in alcohol-related fatalities, he argues.

"The sheer number of lives saved is the important thing to remember," Hon says.

Reform advocates, however, do not believe lower alcohol-related fatalities are directly linked with raising the drinking age. Chafetz says the mere fact that one followed the other does not indicate a definite causal relationship.

But that line of thinking could also be leveled against Engs's numbers on increased violence among heavy drinkers after the age limit was raised—one does not necessarily follow from another. A better argument comes from Engs herself.

"The decrease in drinking and driving problems are the result of many factors and not just the rise in purchase age or the decreased per capita consumption," she writes. "These include: education concerning drunk driving, designated driver programs, increased seat belt and air bag usage, safer automobiles, lower speed limits, free taxi services from drinking establishments, etc."

Pushing for moderation

Designated driver programs make advocates like Hon ambivalent. While they do promote safe driving, Hon says they send the implicit message that as long as one person stays sober, the rest of the group can drink without consequences.

For Marlatt, that line of thinking belies the battle lines in American debates over substance use. No middle ground exists between abstinence (never touching alcohol) and excessiveness (getting wasted every night).

But Marlatt is trying to work out a happy medium. He specializes in "harm reduction." That means working to moderate drinking, without trying to eliminate it right away. Needle exchanges and methadone for heroin users are examples of harm reduction in other drug therapies.

As part of his research, Marlatt conducted a ten-year study of heavy drinkers on college campuses. One group entered a program that included one-on-one sessions about drinking and the negatives associated with the habit.

Students discussed their drinking habits with an interviewer, and their risky behavior was identified. Throughout the interviews, Marlatt says the students were never stigmatized for their drinking. The phrase "You have a problem" was never mentioned. Instead interviewers tried to get students to recognize destructive behavior on their own.

In the short term, students who had the sessions reported drinking less than heavy drinkers who did not go through an interview. Long term alcoholism rates were also higher in the control group.

"[This study] is controversial because we don't insist on abstinence," Marlatt says.

Asked whether he favors lowering the drinking age, the professor demurred, although he did acknowledge the absence of controlled drinking environments for students with a higher age limit. But his study, by avoiding finger pointing, also avoids reactance.

Marlatt's study could serve as a mechanism to open up the drinking age debate to more than just abstinence. And that could be the first step towards bringing the country out of Prohibition for the second time.

6

Repeat Drunk Drivers Are a Threat to Public Safety

Jayne Keedle

Jayne Keedle is a journalist and regular contributor to the Hartford Advocate.

By taking advantage of loopholes in the law or disregarding it altogether, repeat drunk driving offenders are continuing to threaten the safety of other drivers. Repeat offenders operate outside the law by continuing to drive on suspended licenses and without auto insurance coverage. Many chronic drunk drivers are also aware that fleeing the scene of an accident works to their advantage, as blood-alcohol limits must be tested by police within two hours of an accident in order to prove driver intoxication. While the humiliation of being arrested, the loss of a driver's license, and education efforts deter many first-time offenders from continuing to drive drunk, solutions to keeping offenders with persistent drinking problems off the roads remain elusive.

Lawrence Vaughan, 29, was hot and bored, so he did what came naturally to him. He jumped into the red 1979 Cadillac he had bought just two weeks earlier for $200 and turned the key in the ignition. Some might have considered the risks. Vaughan's license, after all, had been suspended as a result of a string of drunk driving convictions. The car was unregistered, uninsured and had stolen plates. But risk was not a worry for Larry Vaughan. His first stop was Super Discount Liquors in his hometown of Waterbury, Connecticut to pick up a 12-pack of beer. From about noon on, he spent the July afternoon driving in aimless circles through Waterbury, Thomaston and onto Route 8, drinking as he cruised. He was still driving as night fell.

Senseless tragedy

At just past 10 P.M., 19-year-old Jason Sumpf, a philosophy student at the University of Connecticut with a passion for poetry, music and restoring

Reprinted from "Blind-Drunk Justice," by Jayne Keedle, *Hartford Advocate*, August 21, 1997. Reprinted with permission from *Hartford Advocate*.

vintage Chevy Novas, was leaving a party at 43 South St. in Plymouth. As he rummaged through his pockets to find the key to his girlfriend's car, headlights flashed across his black shirt. Sumpf was a second degree black belt in karate, but his reflexes weren't quick enough to jump out of the way of the oncoming car. A friend, Jonathan Osowiecki, heard the sickening thump and saw Sumpf's body tumble 15 feet through the air and fall in a heap by the side of the road.

He would later remember Jason's sneaker turning over and over in the air as if in slow motion. Sumpf lay bleeding profusely from a head wound, his broken leg twisted grotesquely beneath him. He warned Jason's girlfriend, Sharon Foley, not to look. The driver never even slowed down.

Chronically drunk drivers are more likely to be involved in fatal accidents and are more likely to flee the scene of an accident than others.

At 11:50 P.M., state police noticed a red 1979 Cadillac Coupe DeVille on the shoulder of Route 8 in Watertown. They pulled over and discovered Vaughan asleep at the wheel. He had apparently run out of gas, but Trooper Mark DeFeo suspected he had been drinking and charged him with driving under the influence with a suspended license. Although the front of the car looked as if it had been in an accident, police in Watertown had no reason to connect Vaughan with the hit-and-run that had occurred in Plymouth earlier that evening.

Sumpf was rushed to Waterbury Hospital. As the teenager lay in critical condition, police asked bystanders and neighbors to come forward with any information that might help them locate the car and driver involved in the accident. As 100 friends and family members held a candlelight vigil for Sumpf Sunday evening at the gazebo in his hometown of Thomaston, police were still looking for leads. Sumpf was pronounced dead at 5 P.M. Monday from extensive head injuries sustained in the accident. On Tuesday, police announced that there might be a connection between the Sumpf's death and the red Coupe DeVille found on Route 8.

Getting off easy

The state forensics lab took four months to confirm that Vaughan's car was, indeed, the one that hit Sumpf. When Sumpf's father, Peter, called the lab to see what was taking so long, he was shocked when the person on the other end of the line asked about his son's health. Shortly thereafter, the lab's analysis of the head-sized dent had matched blood type, tissue and clothing to Jason and directly connected Vaughan's red Cadillac to the fatal accident.

Both Peter Sumpf and Jason's mother, Sue DelBuono, expected the state to throw the book at Vaughan. Initially, however, Patrick McGinley, the state's attorney in Bristol, didn't plan to prosecute the case as a manslaughter at all. McGinley told Sumpf's mother that the charge would be felony evading—legalese for a hit-and-run. DelBuono and Peter Sumpf were at a loss to understand the prosecutor's reasoning. When they contacted Mothers Against Drunk Driving (MADD) to find out how this might have happened, the advocacy group went public with their outrage. The charge against Vaughan failed to acknowledge that Jason Sumpf had been killed. If convicted, Vaughan's maximum sentence would be only five years in prison and a $1,000 fine.

Recently, DelBuono saw Vaughan for the first time in court. "He seems completely a lost cause," she says of the man she believes killed her son. "I remember thinking, 'How could somebody like that destroy someone like Jason?' [My son] walked into a room and the room lit up. He had more things he wanted to achieve than he could have in six lifetimes. I've tried to feel some compassion, but [Vaughan] has been messing up since 1989 and walking away. Why doesn't he get punished?"

The repeat offender menace

That is a question too many other bereaved families in Connecticut have asked themselves. Legislators, law enforcement officials and advocacy groups such as Mothers Against Drunk Driving all agree that chronically drunk drivers are more likely to be involved in fatal accidents and are more likely to flee the scene of an accident than others. But although the law in Connecticut is tough on drunk driving, no one has found a way to keep repeat offenders like Lawrence Vaughan off the roads. Currently, several proposals are before the Legislature that could, at least, keep persistent drunk drivers behind bars for longer periods.

Perversely, however, the very toughness of the legal system seems to conspire to keep drunk drivers in their cars and on the roads. Many persistent offenders are already operating outside the law. They are driving without licenses because their licenses have been suspended and many drive vehicles that are unregistered or whose registration has expired. As a result, they are also driving without insurance, which makes it hard for people involved in accidents with them to sue and get significant compensation.

Flee the scene, avoid prison

The brutal fact is that drunk drivers have more reason to flee the scene of an accident than to stick around. Indeed, the system seems to reward drunk drivers involved in hit-and-run accidents for a simple reason: If blood alcohol limits aren't tested within two hours of the accident, there's no way to prove that the driver was drunk at the time. Like Vaughan, many offenders are familiar with the criminal justice system. They know they won't be referred to the Pretrial Alcohol Education System and emerge with clean records like Oksana Baiul [figure skater arrested for drunk driving in Connecticut in 1997]. They will face prison time instead. This gives them great incentive to flee from accident scenes, possibly leaving behind people with injuries, which may put victims at even greater risk. Moreover, if the drunk drivers have time to disappear and sober up before anyone can test their blood alcohol level, they can escape the lengthier sentences that accompany the charge of vehicular manslaughter or assault coupled with drunk driving.

Prosecutor McGinley, who was finally persuaded by Jason Sumpf's parents to press charges of vehicular manslaughter while driving under the influence against Vaughan, refuses to talk about the details of the case. . . . But he will say that hit-and-run cases, particularly those in which alcohol may have been involved, are difficult to investigate and prosecute for several reasons. "Who do we look for when we find a body by the side of the road?" asks McGinley. "We look for someone who has it in for them. Those pieces don't fit. They don't fall into place."

With no motive to trace, there are few leads. Moreover, because most drunk driving accidents occur late at night, often after bars and package stores are closed, there may be no witnesses to connect the driver to the car. "These present very difficult factual cases," says McGinley. "They're often circumstantial, with no witnesses or witnesses who because of injury suffer amnesia or don't recall, that's just the nature of the offense."

Too many loopholes

DelBuono was shocked when she learned that Vaughan had a long history of driving drunk. Vaughan's record, which dates back to 1989, includes at least two driving while intoxicated (DWI) convictions and several others for driving illegally—as well as convictions for burglary, larceny, trespassing, breach of peace and failing on a number of occasions to appear in court.

The more Jason's mother studied the existing laws, the easier it seemed for chronic drunk drivers to avoid prosecution. If the car wasn't running or the keys weren't in the ignition, a defense lawyer could argue that while their client may have been drunk, no one was driving. By leaving the scene of an accident—therefore avoiding arrest and a blood alcohol test—it's hard to prove that the driver was drunk at the time, even if later police find him stinking of booze. The excuse heard often by law enforcement is that the driver involved was shaken up by the accident and drank to calm down afterwards.

That is, if the driver even acknowledges that there was an accident. Vaughan, for instance, told police he had been drinking and driving, but says he doesn't remember hitting anything.

> *By leaving the scene of an accident . . . it's hard to prove that the driver was drunk at the time.*

Proving a hit-and-run case is harder than proving a homicide, particularly if there are no witnesses to connect a driver to the scene of an accident and no legal papers to suggest that the driver even owns a car. The reality is that many people whose licenses are suspended drive knowing full well that they'll to go to jail for 30 days if they're caught. If they abuse alcohol chronically, however, often they don't even consider the consequences of their actions. "The problem is really when they can't be found for a day or so," says Jack Cronan, executive assistant state's attorney. "The longer the time, the more easily the operator can escape getting arrested."

As DelBuono sees it, Vaughan has learned how to use the system—and it's working to his advantage. "I didn't want to help the system fail," she says. "I'd rather put it on the line and fight to change the system so the next person doesn't have to go through this."

Changing the system is not easy. Currently, a bill proposed by state representatives Lenny Winkler (R-Groton) and Peter Nystrom (R-Norwich) is before the Legislature's Judiciary Committee. It would increase the penalty for drunk drivers convicted in vehicular manslaughter and assault with a motor vehicle who have prior DWI convictions. At the moment, the charge of second degree manslaughter with a motor vehicle while intoxicated carries the toughest penalty. It's a Class C felony, punishable by a term of up to 10 years, a fine of $10,000, or both. Winkler's proposal would increase it to a Class B felony, punishable by up to 20 years in prison, a fine of up to $15,000, or both. She would also like to give judges the option to ensure that repeat offenders who have been involved in serious but not fatal accidents serve at least three years in jail.

Repeat [drunk driving] offenders are more likely to be involved in the most serious accidents than other drivers.

"I put this bill in last year as a result of a constituent in my district. A young boy, Joshua Stewart, was killed by a drunk driver who was a repeat offender," says Winkler. "It would authorize a court to impose an enhanced penalty on a person who had previously been convicted of driving under the influence. We seem to see a lot of them. I'm optimistic we'll be successful at dealing with this year."

Last session Winkler's bill was approved unanimously by the Judiciary Committee, but the session ended before the Legislature had a chance to vote on it. This year, Winkler hopes that the longer legislative session and increased awareness of the problem will be enough to pass the bill. It's certainly on Mothers Against Drunk Driving's lobbying agenda.

Losing ground: hidden numbers of repeat offenders

"It's not the person that left the wedding that's the problem," says Bernie McLoughlin, who works on public policy for Connecticut's chapter of MADD, which he helped found in 1985 after he and his wife were injured in a car accident involving a drunk driver. "It's a pattern of drinking and driving and it finally catches up with them in a tragic way in the end."

Although no one has exact figures on the number of alcohol-related traffic fatalities in which the drivers had prior DWI convictions, at least half a dozen cases of fatal accidents in which the drunk driver was a repeat offender are currently being adjudicated in state courts. The victims include Joshua Stewart, who would have been 16 this year; Darci Hutchinson, a 21-year-old woman from Uncasville; and Jason Sumpf.

Jane Engelke, a member of MADD whose own son was killed in 1984 by a drunk driver who had been arrested for DWI just seven weeks before the fatal accident, suggests that there may be many more repeat offenders involved in accidents than that. She points out that DWI arrests are, after a year, wiped from the records of first-time offenders who participate in the alcohol education program.

"We've made great progress, but there's been a backslide," says McLoughlin. "Unfortunately, fatalities are up for the first time in a decade. The fact that people are dying out there at a higher rate means we've got work to do."

In 1995, fatalities due to drunk driving increased by 41 percent in Connecticut. Of the 72,667 auto accidents recorded in the state that year, 1,990 involved alcohol and 122 of them were fatal, killing 136 people. Tellingly, nearly half of all fatal accidents in Connecticut in 1995 involved alcohol. Research conducted by MADD shows that repeat offenders are more likely to be involved in the most serious accidents than other drivers. And there are plenty of people on the roads today who have been busted at least once for DWI. In 1995, Connecticut courts handled 12,534 drunk-driving cases. Of those arrested, most did not go to jail and their driving records are clean today.

Renewed education efforts

Still, MADD believes that the first line of defense against drunk driving is education. "With the current laws, you always get a second chance, because drunk driving is viewed as an epidemic that can be solved," says McLoughlin. Since 1981, first-time offenders have generally been referred to the Pretrial Alcohol Education System, where, for eight or 10 weeks—depending on their age and blood alcohol level; those underage and with a blood alcohol at .15 percent and above are put in the longer program—they learn about the effects alcohol has on the body and the laws concerning driving under the influence. That, coupled with the humiliation of being arrested and the inconvenience of having their driver's license suspended for at least 30 days (many can and do get permits to drive to and from work), is usually enough to shock people into staying sober behind the wheel.

Cinda Cash, the director of Alcohol Services Organization, Inc., which runs the education program in the New Haven area, is struck by the number of people who don't believe that drinking and driving is a serious offense. Part of the mission of the classes is to press that point home. Most, Cash adds, do get the message. Still, she estimates that 10 percent of them have persistent drinking problems. If they keep driving, their chances of being in a serious accident increase.

"Short of putting someone in jail, there's not too much you can do," says executive assistant state's attorney Cronan. "A person who may have had his license suspended so many times he may never get it back decides to drive anyway." There are 100,000 people in Connecticut whose licenses are currently under suspension.

Searching for solutions

Other MADD proposals may be a harder sell. Lowering the legal blood alcohol level will be an uphill battle. Despite the fact that neighboring states set their limits at .08 percent, adds Cronan, he hasn't seen an abundance of scientific evidence to support it. Prosecutors complain that the DWI laws change too often—just about every year for the past 10 years, in fact—as loopholes are discovered and sealed.

As Oksana Baiul's 1997 accident demonstrated, unless the driver is first arrested, hospital blood tests aren't sufficient for the Department of Motor Vehicles to automatically suspend a driver's license. Blood alcohol levels must be tested within two hours of an accident to prove that the driver is over the .10 percent legal limit. Currently, unless the tests are supervised by police officers, the DMV is not empowered to automatically suspend anyone's driver's license. Legislators with a keen eye on civil rights, however, may not be willing to plug the loophole to allow hospital blood tests taken without police supervision to be used to justify taking away someone's right to drive. Nor is it likely that hospitals would welcome police into their labs, nagging about two-hour time limits while doctors are trying to save critically ill patients.

It's pretty near impossible to stop people with chronic drinking problems from breaking the law by driving.

Both the proposal to lower the legal limit to .08 and close what will probably come to be known as the Oksana Baiul loophole will likely be spearheaded by Sen. Edith Prague (D-Columbia), one of the most active anti–drunk driving legislators in Connecticut.

"I came into the House in 1983 with the promise to do something about drunk driving. My niece was killed by a drunk driver when she was 21 and nothing happened to the driver because there were no laws on the books establishing the level at .10 as the legal limit. We got that established, and that was a battle. The lawyers were fighting that," says Prague. "Little did I think I'd be standing here 10 years later doing the same thing."

Baiul may have exposed a loophole in the current drunk driving laws, but the gap big enough to do a triple axel through is one that legislators and law enforcement agencies may be powerless to close. With inadequate public transportation and a society that reinforces the idea that everyone is entitled to their own car, it's pretty near impossible to stop people with chronic drinking problems from breaking the law by driving.

"What can you do with a repeat offender? How can you get them off the road?" asks Prague. "It's impossible to control this 100 percent. It seems we have to remind people that drinking and driving kills people, devastates families and is avoidable. But the devastation it causes is beyond imagination."

Still waiting for answers

More than 100 people came to the memorial service for Jason Sumpf at Cote's Field in Thomaston. Like his young life, the event was more celebratory than sad. His father Peter strapped on a guitar and played a rock instrumental in honor of Jason, who played rhythm guitar in a local band, Long Road Back. Friends and family wore tie-dye instead of black. They leafed through scrapbooks of photographs and poems that Jason had written. One, in particular, struck a chord:

Life is only worth living if you have love in it
And the only way you can receive love is to earn it.
Enjoy life and love while you have it
Because you never know when life will
Take an odd twist into death.

An odd twist of fate took Jason's life. And, like many parents who have lost a child prematurely, his mother still wonders why. But nowadays her questions are more specific and they're not addressed to God. Why did she practically have to push the prosecutor to charge Vaughan with manslaughter and driving under the influence? Why is a hit-and-run fatality by a drunk driver so hard to prove in court? Whether or not Vaughan is convicted of all the charges he faces remains to be seen.

But the biggest question of all for Sue DelBuono is why was a man with such a long history of driving drunk still on the roads? She wants an answer to that one. She cannot forget that the last words she said to her son were "be careful." Sadly, there was no way Jason could have seen someone like Vaughan coming. But considering Vaughan's driving record, someone should have.

7

A Combination of Legal Sanctions Will Stop Repeat Drunk Drivers

Herb Simpson

Herb Simpson is president and chief executive officer of the Traffic Injury Research Foundation, a road safety institute working to reduce traffic related deaths and injuries.

Individuals who repeatedly drive after consuming large quantities of alcohol, known as the "hard core" of drunk drivers, cause up to 65 percent of serious alcohol-related auto collisions. Many of these chronic drunk drivers have received numerous convictions yet refuse to change their behavior when threatened with standard punishments such as fines, jail, and the loss of a driver's license. In fact, up to 75 percent continue to drive on suspended licenses. Effective remedies for keeping these hard core offenders off the roads include ignition interlock devices, which require the driver to pass a breath test before the car will start, and vehicle seizure for those caught driving with suspended licenses. Most importantly, treatment programs, though a long-term process, are essential for second-time offenders, the majority of whom are alcohol abusers.

D espite the impressive gains that have been made in the fight against drunk driving, a dangerous minority, called the Hard Core, keeps bucking the trend. This group repeatedly takes to road after consuming large amounts of alcohol, placing themselves and others at very great risk. They often have blood alcohol concentrations (BACs) that are double or triple the legal limit, causing a majority of drinking and driving deaths.

Tragic consequences

As a result, they continue to make headlines in the most regrettable way: A Florida man was convicted of driving under the influence (DUI)

Reprinted from "Drunk, Dangerous, and Deadly: Who Are Hard Core Drunk Drivers and What Should Be Done to Get Them Off the Nation's Roads," by Herb Simpson, speech delivered to the American Legislative Exchange Council's annual meeting, Nashville, TN, August 12, 1999.

manslaughter in the deaths of five people. He had a BAC of .25—a level that is two and a half times the legal limit in most states. His license had been suspended and even revoked in three states for prior drinking and driving offenses.

Or consider the case of a North Carolina man who was recently convicted of second-degree murder in the death of a young woman who was a sophomore in college and also the mother of a two-year-old. He had a BAC of .26 and had two previous drunk driving convictions.

In another tragic case, a 31-year-old Tennessee woman and her unborn child were killed when a drunk driver ran his truck up on a curb, pinning the woman against a light pole. The man driving the car had a BAC of .28. His license had already been revoked because of two previous drunk driving convictions.

Recognizing the threat to public safety

Unfortunately, these are not rare, isolated events but all too familiar. However, it is only in recent years that hard core drinking drivers have received serious attention from policy makers. Contemporary focus on the problem began in the U.S. at the beginning of the 1990s with the publication of what has become an internationally acclaimed study entitled, *The Hard Core Drinking Driver*. Conducted by the Traffic Injury Research Foundation (TIRF), under a grant from Anheuser-Busch, this research documented the extent of the problem caused by this group and identified it as a target for special attention by policy leaders.

Several years later, TIRF, again with support from Anheuser-Busch, provided a comprehensive review of effective and promising programs and policies for dealing with hard core drinking drivers. This study urged lawmakers to better enforce laws already on the books and use proven methods to deal with these troublemakers.

Since then, many organizations, both public and private, have joined the fight in dealing with these extremely dangerous drivers. Recognition is growing not only of the severe threat they pose to public safety but the challenge they present. This is underscored by the fact that they have numerous convictions. This is a double-edged sword from a public policy standpoint. The system is obviously having some success because hard core drinking drivers keep getting caught; at the same time, the system is failing because the same offenders are frequently caught again and again. Obviously, they are not receptive to traditional appeals and are even resistant to changing their behavior in the face of the usual sanctions. New approaches are needed.

Identifying the "hard core"

In part, the challenge presented by this group lies in identifying them. Studies have shown that the hard core represents less than one percent of all nighttime drivers. Being such a small group, it can be very challenging to target them through traditional enforcement.

However, this small group is a significant threat, causing as many as 65 percent of the serious collisions. The major reason for this is that they drive with very high BACs, which has a profound effect on their risk of being in a serious traffic accident. A driver with a BAC of .20 or higher is 460 times more likely to be involved in a fatal crash than a driver with no alcohol, or very low amounts of alcohol, in their system.

But, as indicated earlier, the hard core does fall into the arms of the criminal justice system with great regularity, so it is imperative that the most be made of these opportunities to address them with effective policies. And, research shows that there are very real limits to the ability of stiffer monetary fines and longer jail sentences to induce changes in their drinking and driving behavior. Fortunately, there is an emerging consensus that the strategic application of a diversity of proven measures can have a significant positive impact. And, there are proven measures at our disposal. Let me briefly describe a few of them.

What can be done?

At the top of the list is rehabilitation. Because so many of the hard core are alcohol abusers or dependent—up to 75% of second time offenders, there is a need to get offenders into treatment. To ensure that officials prescribe the most appropriate treatment for offenders, a reliable screening and assessment technique should be used to identify the nature and severity of their problems.

And, treatment works. It has a significant impact on re-offense rates and alcohol-related crashes. But a note of caution is warranted. Because it is a long-term process and by no means perfectly effective, treatment should be provided in combination with other sanctions and not used as a substitute for, or a means to circumvent them.

It is only in recent years that hard core drinking drivers have received serious attention from policy makers.

One of those other sanctions is license suspension. It has been one of the most popular and effective sanctions for drunk driving. However, many offenders are not deterred by the loss of their license; up to 75% drive anyway. And, some continue to drink and drive. This behavior can be remarkably persistent. For example, a motorist in New York City was recently stopped making an illegal U-turn. During this, the police discovered the driver was the "phantom motorist" whose license had been suspended 633 times since 1990. This motorist had eluded capture for four years, and it took the computer nearly two hours to generate a written report of the motorist's driving record.

Vehicle-based sanctions

For such hard core offenders, the next logical step is to deny them access to their vehicle, or to ensure that if they do drive, they have not been drinking. Actions against the vehicle have been gaining in popularity in the past few years.

In general, these vehicle-based measures are designed to limit the mobility of the offender. At one end of the spectrum is the alcohol-ignition interlock, a device that still allows the offender and their family to use the vehicle but only if they are sober. At the other end of the spectrum is vehicle immobilization, which denies the offender and family access to the vehicle.

The ignition interlock is a small breath test device installed in the vehicle to measure the driver's BAC. The driver is required to provide a zero or low-BAC breath sample to operate the vehicle. Technological improvements in these devices over the past several decades prevent virtually all of the known ways to "fool" the system.

This small group [of hard core drinking drivers] is a significant threat, causing as many as 65 percent of the serious collisions.

Ignition interlocks work. Evaluation studies have consistently demonstrated that interlocks are effective—the re-arrest rate among offenders with an interlock device has been found to be as much as 75% lower than among those without the device.

Obviously with an interlock on the vehicle, family members and the offender can drive it. But some vehicle sanctions allow only the family to use it, not the offender. These typically involve special license plates, such as blaze-orange or zebra-striped, primarily to alert police to the fact that this is the vehicle of a convicted drunk driver. Ideally, the legislation that permits the use of these plates empowers the police to stop such a vehicle and verify that the driver is not the offender.

The most severe form of vehicle-based sanctions includes immobilization or impoundment, and forfeiture. Depending on the jurisdiction, the vehicle can be seized by the police if the driver is under suspension for any reason, or for an alcohol-related offense, or is driving under the influence of alcohol. The vehicle is then either placed in a secure compound for a period of usually one or two months or it is immobilized with a device such as a "club" on the steering wheel, often in the offender's driveway.

No single solution

There is solid evidence that these programs have a significant impact on the prevalence of driving while under suspension as well as on alcohol related collisions. In Canada, a federally-funded study by TIRF showed there was a 12 percent decrease in drunk driving fatalities when vehicles are impounded, along with a 50 percent decrease in DUI offenses. Most importantly, there was a 27 percent decrease in repeat driving while suspended offenses, a category that many hard core drinking drivers fall into. Evaluations of programs in California, Ohio and Minnesota have also produced positive results.

The toughest vehicle sanction program was introduced in New York City in 1999. The ordinance began making headlines because the vehicle of anyone stopped for drunk driving, most of whom do not fit the hard core drunk driving description, was seized and forfeited. This very aggressive approach has not yet been evaluated but the attention the law has gathered, from both fans and critics, underscores an important lesson we should not forget in dealing with this problem. Too frequently countermeasures are embraced as the silver bullet, magic elixir or panacea for the problem. If we have learned one lesson in the long struggle to deal with this problem it is that there is no single solution, it requires a diversity of complementary measures. License suspension became for many "the solution" of the 80s; hopefully, vehicle forfeiture will not become "the solution" of the 90s. Both work but they are only part of the puzzle.

Drinking and driving declined dramatically during the 1980s and continued to show some, albeit more modest, progress in the 90s. Many have argued that we've already achieved the easy gains because responsible, social drinkers have gotten the message. Hard core drinking drivers have not. Many do not care about the threat they pose to others, or even about being punished. Many keep drinking and driving when their license is suspended. They are the single largest challenge in the continuing battle against impaired driving and must be a priority if further meaningful progress is to be made. A key to that progress is the widespread use of effective measures for dealing with hard core drinking drivers.

8

Ignition Interlock Devices Prevent Drunk Driving

Darrel L. Longest

Darrel L. Longest is the founder and CEO of Life Sciences Corporation, a privately held company known as the Ignition Interlock Group. The company is a multi-state service provider for ignition interlocks that installs, maintains, monitors, and reports on interlock use by DUI and DWI offenders.

Ignition interlock devices prevent drunk driving offenders from operating motor vehicles while intoxicated by requiring a breath test from the driver before the vehicle will start. The devices also contain computer chips that record drivers' attempts to drive drunk. Interlock devices have been proven to reduce the re-arrest rates of chronic drunk driving offenders, who participate in ignition interlock programs on a voluntary basis in exchange for early driver's license reinstatement after a conviction. States are expanding their use of ignition interlock programs under pressure from Congress, which is threatening to withhold highway construction funds from states if high risk offenders are not more successfully treated. Due to their effectiveness, and to their ability to provide valuable information about driver behavior, ignition interlock programs should begin to play a larger role in the battle against drunk driving.

For those not familiar with interlock programs, they have a Breathalyzer® device that is hard-wired into the ignition system of any vehicle and requires a breath test before the vehicle will start, which documents the driver's attempts to drink and drive. To prevent the use of "curbside" help from a friend, anti-circumvention measures are built into the breath testing process, along with a "rolling retest" that requires a random breath test about 3 times each hour while driving. There are now 39 states with laws that permit the use of these programs, and more are pending legislation this year.[1] Interlock programs are offender-supported, depending on no tax money.

Excerpted from "What's New in the Ignition Interlock World?" by Darrel L. Longest. www. ignitioninterlock.com/impaired.htm. Copyright © 2000 Life Sciences Corporation. Originally published by *Civic Research Foundation, Impaired Driving Update.* Reprinted with permission.

Interlock studies show continuing success

Ignition interlock programs have made large strides in the US and abroad since 1998.

The University of Maryland study of April 1997 by Beck, Rauch & Baker ("The Effects of Alcohol Ignition Interlock License Restrictions on Multiple Alcohol Offenders: A Randomized Trial in Maryland," *Proceedings of the 14th International Conference on Alcohol, Drugs, and Traffic Safety*, vol. 1, pp. 177–92 [Annecy, France CERMT, Centre d'Etudes et de Recherches on Medecine du Trafic]), has been subjected to a number of reviews, including a study reported in the *American Journal of Preventive Medicine*, (Coben & Larkin [1999], "Effectiveness of Ignition Interlock Devices in Reducing Drunk Driving Recidivism," AJPM, 16, pp. 81–87). Interlocks have been found to be very effective in reducing recidivism amongst offenders with an average of 3.5 convictions (65% reduction in this group, with a year's interlock program).

Additional research has added strength to the earlier studies concerning the ability of interlock devices to reduce re-arrest rates in the family of hard-core, persistent drinking drivers. Dr. Robert Voas, *et. al.*, of the Pacific Institute for Research has published twice on the subject of the role of interlocks.[2] Voas has found the interlock to be very useful in reducing recidivism, but that their ability to have a greater impact on recidivism could be much larger if they were in greater use, since only a small percentage of offenders will volunteer to have an early license reinstatement with an interlock program.

It is clearer now than in 1998 that, while interlocks are not a panacea, or the "Silver Bullet," for solving our drinking and driving problem, they are a very successful tool not only to reduce recidivism while they are being used, but after their use, if they are utilized in treatment programs that know how to read and interpret the datalogger information produced from interlock devices.

The success of these studies has settled one long-term question that was previously answered only by anecdotal evidence: Are interlocks effective in reducing drinking and driving? They clearly are. The questions now are: What is the model program protocol, and how do we get the most from these programs? We will examine here what a few states are doing to make interlock programs work better for them.

Development of a model interlock program

Progress: We are well on our way to development of a model interlock program. Several states with well-established programs have taken a close look at how they can get more from their interlock programs, and others have followed their example; there are several who have done little in this regard, and need to do so before their programs will be successful.

All but the very oldest of interlock devices now have a "datalogger"—a memory chip that records information from the interlock, such as the value and time of each breath alcohol test taken, the number of engine starts in each monitoring period (usually every 30 days), hours of operation, and many other bits of information useful in monitoring probation and rehabilitation progress and compliance.

Now, more than at any other time, virtually all state authorities have realized that an interlock program involves not merely the installation of an interlock device, but the entire protocol that comes with it—how it is to be installed, security issues, how often it is to be serviced and calibrated and the data removed from the device, and what information will be transmitted to the monitoring authorities so that they may use it in the rehabilitation and probation process to monitor driver behavior while on the interlock program. Many of the better statewide interlock programs are now using the valuable information about driver behavior stored in the interlock's datalogger, requiring service providers to provide that information in carefully developed computer programs and even in an electronic format for delivery to probation, treatment, research, and Department of Motor Vehicles (DMV) authorities (e.g., Virginia, Maryland, West Virginia, and Tennessee). Some have actually established enforcement procedures that keep providers on their toes, providing higher level services than in states without any regulation of providers or manufacturers, and enforcing them by field inspections.

Others have expanded their use of interlock programs, but without yet establishing higher-level requirements for devices or for service providers (e.g., Texas, Oklahoma, New Mexico, and Washington State). All this has added to the level of comfort for courts, probation and DMV authorities to use interlock devices, although the states without good service and device protocols are still groping for the right combinations of these regulations. Once they have these requirements added to their protocols, there will be an even higher level of confidence in the programs.

Challenges to developing interlock programs

Although there has been movement in developing sound interlock programs and requiring service providers to meet certain minimum standards to qualify to install, calibrate, monitor and report on interlock use, there remains opposition by some manufacturers and providers to doing so, as change is expensive to adopt, and some are seeking to get all they can out of older equipment, at the expense of the driving public.

> *While interlocks are not a panacea, or the "Silver Bullet," for solving our drinking and driving problem, they are a very successful tool.*

There are now many manufacturers of interlock devices. All but 2 of these now make an alcohol-specific interlock device, which will not render positives to such things as cigarette smoke or foods. Although many states have put a stop to the use of older equipment, and are requiring the use of the alcohol-specific devices to reduce the "false positives" that occur in the use of older equipment, some have been reluctant to require newer technology to be used. Thus, false positives still exist in the field, and will remain until the state authorities demand that better technology (readily available) be used.

There has been no movement in another difficult area. There are still no commonly accepted qualifications for the laboratories that test interlock devices. Although some have adopted a requirement that an ISO-9000 [International Organization for Standardization—international standards that apply to electronics] qualified lab, or a state crime lab (e.g., Virginia and Nevada) do the independent evaluation of interlock device test results to see that they pass the National Highway Traffic Safety Administration (NHTSA) guidelines for technical requirements, there are still those that will accept nearly any lab's certification, and even some that still allow "self-certification" by a manufacturer. The states need to adopt regulations that will mandate testing by a qualified state crime lab or a private lab that is either ISO-9000 certified, or certified to some internationally recognized requirement that will ensure that a reliable product goes into the field. In 1998, some members of the International Association of Chemical Testers (IACT) asked NHTSA to have interlocks tested by the Volpe Labs under NHTSA supervision, but no action on that suggestion has occurred yet. NHTSA should move on this suggestion, and all the "hoop-la" over which devices do, and do not, meet the NHTSA guidelines—and the acrimony that goes with it—will go away.

We are well on our way to development of a model interlock program.

There continues to be a wide variance in interlock device sensor stability, with some devices (usually those with the "T" cell) going out of calibration well within a 30 day monitoring period, and others staying very stable over long periods of time (well in excess of 90 days). Requiring an alcohol-specific sensor that will be stable for longer terms, tested by a qualified lab, will also eliminate this sensor instability problem, prevent false positive results, and increase the courts' and DMVs' willingness to use interlocks.

The biggest challenge remains: to describe and implement the optimum combination of interlock device and program protocols (the age-old questions: who is eligible, how long should the interlock be used, what kinds of reports should be provided, what are the technical requirements of a good program, what information is fed to the treatment programs, and what do you do with the offender who continues to drink and tries—even though unsuccessfully—to drive?). Many states are homing in on the right formula, and several organizations looked at this topic in 2000 (through more independent studies, and education by Mothers Against Drunk Driving (MADD), NHTSA, and the National Commission Against Drunk Driving [NCADD]).

Interlocks, MADD, and the federal government

Perhaps the longest strides in the interlock world in 1999 have come in the recent actions taken by Congress, NHTSA, and MADD. The successful studies of interlock programs and the problem of the "higher risk driver" have not escaped the eye of MADD-National and the federal government.

Always vigilant to the problem of the persistent drinking driver, in 1998, the Transportation Equities Act of the 21st Century (TEA-21) was passed. In addition to providing billions of dollars during the next 5 years for highway, bridge and mass transit construction, it provides for a number of highway safety programs to be enacted by the states.

In prior years, Congress has merely encouraged the states to engage in safety programs to deal with the DUI/DWI multiple offender. Now, they have outlined a specific group of programs that the states must adopt to fight this offender, *under penalty of having some of their construction funds diverted by the federal government into safety programs.* Under the watchful eye of NHTSA, Congress included ignition interlock programs as one of these programs. Starting in October 2000, every state will lose some portion of its construction funding to highway safety programs unless they adopt, among other things, a vehicle impoundment, confiscation, *or* ignition interlock program for the multiple offender.

In late December 1999, MADD and NHTSA held a press conference in Washington. The topic was a newly-coined phrase, the "Higher Risk Driver Program." This is a DUI/DWI offender who has a blood alcohol concentration (BAC) at arrest of 0.16% or higher, or any multiple offender within 5 years. Although there are many facets to the MADD program that do not directly involve the use of interlocks, MADD has set out a program of compromises that utilizes the benefits of interlock programs in the following ways:

1. The Higher Risk Driver is a person with a second DUI within a 5-year period, or a first offender DUI with a BAC of 0.16% or higher, or a driving while suspended offender, where the suspension was the result of a conviction for DUI.

2. For repeat offenders, there will be:
   a. 1-year hard administrative license suspension, and a 2-year suspension for refusal to take a breath test at arrest.
   b. 60-day immobilization or impoundment of the vehicle driven at the time of arrest.
   c. A 5-year period during which the offender is subject to a 0.15% BAC level and provide breath tests upon request.
   d. Ignition interlock program for license reinstatement, to remain in the program for 1 year.

3. For the High BAC Drivers (whether first or multiple offense):
   a. Hard license suspension period greater than the suspension for under a 0.16%, with a 2-year suspension for refusal to take the test.
   b. Ignition interlock device required prior to issuance of probationary, hardship, or work permit license and for the full license suspension period.

4. For the driver caught while driving on a license suspended as a result of a DUI or DWI conviction:
   a. Ignition interlock required for the remaining li-

cense suspension period and any additional suspension period imposed as a result of the conviction for driving while suspended.
b. A 1-month vehicle impoundment or immobilization for the first offense, with forfeiture for any sub-
sequent offenses.

Although portions of this program, which was fully supported during the
press conference by the Acting Administrator of NHTSA, will no doubt
run into some problems with several state legislatures (many do not like
the concept of vehicle impoundment or confiscation due to the hardship
that it places on many families, and the fact that there are often many ex-
ceptions that result in the release of vehicles), there can be little doubt
that with the backing of MADD and the financial consequences of TEA-
21's multiple offenders programs bearing down on state highway construction budgets, there will be a vastly expanded use of interlocks starting in 2000.

Interlocks and the private sector

Corporate America has a high-risk paradox on its hands, even without
their employees being charged with a DUI.

Here's how it comes about: Many businesses provide for substantial
health care and employee assistance for those in need of alcohol and or
drugs of abuse help (called Employee Assistance Programs, or EAP). Thus,
the corporation's Personnel Department, Human Resources, or Health Officer becomes aware of the extent of these problems. Management does
not want to fire a good employee who has been there for many years, is
a good worker, and is productive, whether they have a known driving-
related alcohol problem, or not.

---

*There can be little doubt that . . . there will be a
vastly expanded use of interlocks starting in 2000.*

It costs a lot of money to find, hire and train a replacement, and most
major organizations, such as utilities, government fleets, and other high-
maintenance business, would rather try to help cure the problem than
fire the employee. However, if they keep the employee and allow him to
drive on company time, for company business, whether in a personal car
or a company vehicle, the business has an expanded legal exposure for
crashes resulting from the use of alcohol or other drugs of abuse. The
greater the knowledge of the problem, the greater the legal exposure for
allowing the alcohol-related driving to occur.

Several companies facing this paradox have turned to interlocks to
help solve it. Interlocks installed in the vehicle that is used during work
have proved to be exceptionally successful in stopping an employee from
drinking and driving on the job. Thousands of jobs have already been
saved by the use of interlocks, while the roads have remained safe for the
driving public at the same time.

Although the major users of interlocks for this purpose remains with the small fleets worried about their liability and driver safety, the interlock's future holds even more room for interlock use in the commercial and private sectors than it does in the realm of DUI offenders, especially among the larger corporate trucking fleets with a high need for compliant data reporting systems. The interlock provides this means. Use of interlock devices, combined with wireless transmission of data and other information useful to the trucking companies on driver and truck performance, will prove to be the easiest way for corporate America to comply with the requirements of the Department of Transportation for random breath alcohol tests and avoid significant sanctions against the driver.

This is the present world of the ignition interlock—one in which studies proving their substantial contribution to reduced recidivism, increased road safety, maintenance of job opportunities, and compliance with federal and state regulations for monitoring of commercial drivers have all come to a junction. 2000 will surely be known as the watershed year for the interlock industry.

Notes

1. A detailed description of interlock programs in nearly every US jurisdiction appears in a paper by Darrel L. Longest, JD, *Administrative and Judicial Interlock Programs in the US*, Proceedings of the Australasian Conference on Drugs Strategy, April, 1999. Pitfalls and solutions are extensively discussed in this paper. A copy is available by emailing www.ignitioninterlock.com.

2. A. Voas, Marques, Tippets & Beirness, "The Alberta Interlock Program: The Evaluation of a Province-Wide Program on DUI Recidivism," *Addiction*, (1999) 94(12), pp. 1849–59;

   B. Marques, Voas, Tippetts, & Beirness, "Behavioral Monitoring of DUI Offenders with the Alcohol Ignition Interlock Recorder," *Addiction*, (1999) 94(12), pp. 1861–70.

9

Sobriety Checkpoints and Blanket Patrols Reduce Alcohol-Related Crashes

National Hardcore Drunk Driver Project

The National Hardcore Drunk Driver Project was created by the Century Council, a national, not-for-profit organization, to provide a comprehensive resource to assist in reducing the number of fatalities, injuries, and damage caused by chronic drunk drivers.

Sobriety checkpoints and blanket patrols are two effective methods used by police to deter and identify drunk drivers. At sobriety checkpoints, police officers conduct face-to-face examinations of motorists to determine whether drivers are intoxicated or driving on suspended licenses due to a prior drunk driving conviction. The majority of states allow checkpoints, and research has shown that overall, checkpoint programs deter potential offenders and reduce alcohol-related crashes and fatalities. Blanket patrols involve officers concentrating on a given area for a set period of time with the goal of spotting and apprehending drunk drivers. These patrols are not limited by law as to the number of officers allowed to participate, giving them an advantage over sobriety checkpoints, which are subject to legal restrictions. In certain jurisdictions, well-publicized blanket patrols have reduced alcohol-related crashes by 60 percent.

S obriety checkpoints, a widely used method for deterring drunk drivers, are a very visible way to deter potential offenders as well as to catch violators. In most states, officers at a checkpoint may examine the license of every driver, or a random sample of drivers. The face-to-face examination allows the police officer to assess whether the driver has been drinking, and it provides an opportunity to apprehend hardcore drunk drivers who generally have a higher alcohol tolerance and, despite high blood alcohol concentration (BAC) levels, may have modified their driving behavior to avoid detection by police officers.[1] Sobriety checkpoints also provide an opportunity to detect people driving with a suspended or revoked driver's license due to a drunk-driving conviction. Sobriety checkpoints require safety cones and special signs and lights that alert the public that the police activity is a sobriety checkpoint. As with blanket patrols, this technique is more effective when highly publicized.

Where are sobriety checkpoints used?

Thirty-nine states and the District of Columbia permit sobriety checkpoints. Even though sobriety checkpoints, when properly conducted, do not violate the U.S. Constitution, approximately ten states prohibit any type of sobriety checkpoint. The most common reason is that the state interprets its constitution as giving more protection against unreasonable searches and seizures than given by the federal constitution. In states that allow sobriety checkpoints, many have their own guidelines which supplement the federal guidelines. Some examples of checkpoint operations follow.

In Tennessee, patrol officers say—Checkpoint Tennessee—is an effective tactic for getting drunk drivers off the roads. Each of the Tennessee Highway Patrol's eight districts conducts sobriety checkpoints monthly. The program uses four specially equipped DUI vans that are outfitted with intoxilyzers, safety lights designed to meet checkpoint regulations, and inside and outside video cameras to document the actions of offenders and officers. The state has found that the vans greatly improve efficiency, resulting in fewer officer hours to establish and maintain checkpoints. In May 1997, the Tennessee Supreme Court ruled that the DUI roadblocks, properly conducted, are constitutional and can continue to be used.

Illinois has deployed two Breath Alcohol Testing (BAT) mobiles that they use as a form of roaming sobriety checkpoints. The vehicles have evidentiary breath-testing capability. They also have an on-board detention facility with a capacity of eight people. The approximate cost per BAT mobile is $67,000.

In San Diego, California, high-profile driving while intoxicated (DWI) enforcement and sobriety checkpoints, used as part of the city's Drunk Driving Enforcement Program, resulted in a 34 percent reduction of alcohol-related crashes. During 1992–93, the use of specialized sobriety checkpoint trailers reduced the average set-up time from thirty minutes to ten minutes, reducing cost, increasing officer safety, and allowing for the operation of checkpoints at multiple locations each night.

How effective are sobriety checkpoints?

During the first two years of a well-publicized sobriety and safety-belt checkpoint program in Binghamton, N.Y., the number of drivers stopped who had been drinking dropped about 40 percent and late-night crashes decreased 21 percent.[2]

A project to study the effectiveness of well-publicized sobriety checkpoint programs found that, as a whole, checkpoint programs reduced alcohol-involved crashes. A 1994 study by the Tennessee Highway Safety Office found that sobriety checkpoints resulted in a 3 percent decline in alcohol-related fatalities. Checkpoint programs in Florida, New Jersey, and Virginia have resulted in significant reductions in alcohol-related crashes.

Some professionals argue that the value of checkpoints can't be measured by arrests alone because one purpose of frequent checkpoints is to increase public awareness of the enforcement programs and deter potential offenders. One example of this results from a 1984 study of two neighboring jurisdictions. Fairfax County, Virginia, had a long history of rigorously enforcing drunk-driving laws and used unpublicized drunk-driver patrols to achieve relatively high arrest rates. Nearby Montgomery County, Maryland, had historically lower arrest rates but used well-publicized sobriety checkpoints during the study period. Surveys of licensed drivers showed that public awareness of enforcement programs was much greater in Montgomery County and that respondents in both counties incorrectly believed they were more likely to be arrested in Montgomery County.[2]

Blanket patrols

Also called saturation patrols, roaming patrols, or dedicated police patrols, blanket patrols are specifically designed to identify drunk drivers. These campaigns are often characterized by a large number of officers concentrating their patrol time on a given area for a set time period. During that time, the police officers stop drivers for any traffic offense, but usually with a particular focus on drunk driving. If well publicized, such patrols serve as general deterrence to drunk drivers. According to the National Hardcore Drunk Driver Project Survey, blanket patrols are used in thirty-nine states and one jurisdiction.

Blanket patrols have been successful in obtaining arrests and enhancing public awareness of enforcement efforts. Measured in arrests per working-hour, a dedicated police patrol is viewed as the most effective method of apprehending offenders. Blanket patrols can offer greater staffing flexibility than sobriety checkpoints, where legal criteria determine the number of personnel required. However, because this technique requires intensive dedication of manpower over a geographic area, it can be impractical for jurisdictions with small police forces and/or large territories.

In Flint, Michigan, the Holiday Operating Under the Influence of Liquor (OUIL) with Media Blitz Enforcement Project used blanket patrols of two traffic sergeants and eight officers for two holiday periods (New Year's 1994 and St. Patrick's Day 1995) at a cost of $5,000. Alcohol-related crashes were reduced by 60 percent compared with the same time periods the previous year.

Notes

1. Martin, S.E., and Preusser, D.F. 1995. *Enforcement strategies for the persistent drinking driver*, Strategies for Dealing with the Persistent Drinking Driver, Transportation Research Board, Transportation Research Circular No. 437. Washington, D.C. National Research Council: 38–42.

2. Insurance Institute for Highway Safety. August 1996. *Alcohol Q&A: Deterrence & Enforcement.* Insurance Institute for Highway Safety.

10

Sobriety Checkpoints Are Unconstitutional

Stephen G. Michaelides

Stephen G. Michaelides is an editorial specialist in foodservice industry publications and was the editor of Restaurant Hospitality *for twenty-one years. He is president of Words, Ink, a business-to-business communications company based in Cleveland, Ohio.*

Mothers Against Drunk Driving (MADD) is wrong in its assertion that sobriety checkpoints are an effective means to combat drunk driving. Checkpoints allow the police to indiscriminately stop drivers for questioning, ignoring their constitutional right to be protected from unreasonable search and seizure and to be accused of a crime only with probable cause. By violating these basic protections, checkpoints set a dangerous precedent for further police infringement on privacy. In addition, checkpoints are ineffective because only a small percentage of drunk drivers are apprehended by them. Police efforts will never bring an end to drunk driving.

I watched this Mothers Against Drunk Driving (MADD) person argue sobriety checkpoints on television a couple of weeks ago, upstaged by sycophantic *legalistas*, and I cringed. I read her declarations in the press—pronouncements as repugnant as oligarchian manifestos—and she offended me more. The entire scenario reminded me of that dreadful show Geraldo Rivera produced a couple of years ago—"Live from Miami, It's Saturday Night Search and Seizure." Remember? Rivera follows a gaggle of cops as they honk their way into homes of suspected drug-dealers/users and at gunpoint uncover *nada*.

Unreasonably MADD

MADD is upset. No big deal there. MADD is *always* upset, and rightfully so, I say. Who out there disputes its goals? Is MADD opposed to drinking? Nope. How about getting drunk? Not even that, although nowadays, anyone condoning *that* risks censure.

MADD is a formidable force, deriving its energy from an intelligence well-nigh irrefutable; i.e., people who drink too much must not drive and if they do, must be punished—not wrist-slapped, but *punished*: paralyzing fines, jail sentences, suspension of license for a long time, maybe forever. Bravo MADD. Onward. Drunk drivers, MADD says, are a menace, often killers and maimers; the sooner we drive them from the streets, the safer the streets will be for everybody.

[Sobriety checkpoints] violate an individual's rights guaranteed under the Constitution.

In the past, MADD's voice has always been tempered with reason, rising above the clamorous babel of neo-prohibitionist fanatics. Not the case, of late. Recent actions would lead one to conclude that MADD has taken leave of its senses. Some members have begun to sound like certain super-patriots I've read about who have tried to contravene constitutional guarantees in order to accommodate their agendas.

Ignoring the Constitution

I refer, of course, to recent developments—given plenty of play in the press—regarding sobriety checkpoints. I have no quarrel with MADD or any other organization that opposes drunk driving. What I do find repugnant are procedures that violate an individual's rights guaranteed under the Constitution, specifically the Fourth Amendment which "protects the people against unreasonable search and seizure."

Roadblocks, checkpoints—whatever—that indiscriminately stop anyone in a motor vehicle for questioning not only ignore probable cause (another guarantee under the Fourth Amendment, which, by the way, insists on "warrants supported by oath"), but call to mind similar strategies employed in police states.

Further, checkpoints don't work. Inasmuch as cops can't eliminate speeding (scofflaws are everywhere), cop-manned checkpoints—erected randomly outside of taverns or restaurants—won't put an end to drunk driving. They can't even hope to curtail it.

Presume for the moment they're perfectly legal. Deal now with the realities of enforcement. How many checkpoints will you need? Where are you going to put them (outside of Spago, of Chi Chi's?)? How many cops will you need? Who's going to pay for all of this? You? Me? MADD?

Frightening hypocrisy

What next? SWAT teams storming bars, guns drawn, sniffing breaths, eyeballing tabs ("Hey, check this one out, Harry, he's been drinking for *days*"), and then confiscating the car keys of those they presume are too drunk to drive? Cops barricading the driveways of homes hosting cocktail parties?

Our politicians squawk out of both sides of their mouths. They condemn inebriation, yet sponsor bills to raise funds for pet projects through "sintaxes."

MADD? Likewise hypocritical. Its challenge is to educate and advise; and, with an energy that reinforces its convictions, to make sure the media covers its activities. That's it. Today, however, it's become an arm of the law, engaging in malpractices that ignore constitutional guarantees.

In much the same way televangelists rely on base sensationalism to whip followers into a fund-raising frenzy, so has MADD allowed its emotions to preempt its common sense, hoping, therefore, to drum up support for its cause. No dice. It has lost mine.

11

Police Use of Passive Alcohol Sensors Deters Drunk Driving

Michele Fields

Michele Fields is general counsel for the Insurance Institute for Highway Safety, a research group funded by auto insurers for the purpose of reducing highway crash deaths, injuries, and property losses.

Passive alcohol sensors (PAS) are devices incorporated into standard police flashlights that measure the approximate amount of alcohol in a person's system. Police officers working at sobriety checkpoints or making traffic stops need only hold the PAS device six to eight inches from a driver while the driver is speaking to determine whether that person has been drinking. Because up to half of all drunk drivers stopped at sobriety checkpoints go undetected, instituting PAS devices as standard police procedure would result in the detection of more drunk drivers. The use of these sensors does not violate the right to privacy under the Constitution, and their powerful deterrent effect on potential drunk drivers would make the roads safer.

The most effective programs to reduce alcohol-impaired driving involve well-publicized enforcement, including sobriety checkpoints. The visibility of checkpoints increases the deterrent effect of driving under the influence (DUI) laws, but as many as 50 percent or more of drivers with high blood alcohol concentrations (BAC) are not identified at checkpoints using traditional enforcement techniques.

Identifying drunk drivers

Police at sobriety checkpoints look for indicators suggestive of a high BAC, such as the odor of alcohol or slow responses to an officer's questions or directions. The presence of these indicators leads officers to look for other signs of a high BAC. So why are officers missing so many high-

Excerpted from Michele Fields, "Yes PAS Give Police an Effective Detection Tool," Washington Post.com, "Issue Forum: Drunk Driving," produced by the Advertising Department of the *Washington Post.*

BAC drivers? One reason is that officers have only a brief time to evaluate drivers at checkpoints and many impaired drivers can hide any overt symptoms for this brief amount of time.

Police officers need an objective way to determine quickly whether a driver has been drinking and approximately how much, and many research studies show that passive alcohol sensors do exactly this. Police can also improve checkpoint efficiency and fairness by decreasing the time spent with drivers who have not been drinking. A recent study found that police working without passive sensors would detain only about 40 to 50 percent of drivers with BACs of .10 percent or higher, while police using passive sensors would detain about 75 percent of these drivers.

Incorporated into a standard police flashlight, a passive alcohol sensor consists of a pump that draws in a sample of ambient air, a fuel cell that reacts to alcohol, and a display indicating the approximate amount of alcohol in the sample. An officer holds the sensor 6 to 8 inches from a driver and takes the sample while the driver is speaking. The driver does not blow into the sensor. Officers may use this method on every driver passing through a checkpoint or at a stop for a traffic violation.

A reliable and legal tool

Is it legal to use sensors? Passive sensors sample the ambient air around a driver's mouth and indicate only the presence and approximate amount of alcohol. This is essentially the same thing officers have been doing, legally, for decades, but sensors are much more reliable than officers' noses.

If a passive sensor indicates no alcohol is present, no further DUI investigation is needed. But if a sensor reading or other signs suggest a high BAC, a driver can be detained for further investigation, and arrested if the investigation warrants it.

As many as 50 percent or more of drivers with high blood alcohol concentrations (BAC) are not identified at checkpoints using traditional enforcement techniques.

Our Constitution protects us against unreasonable searches and seizures. In determining whether a search is legal, courts look at whether police have entered an area that society regards as private, such as the confines of our home. In contrast, the Constitution does not protect what is routinely and freely displayed to the public, such as the sound of our voice, the way we look and walk, or our odor. In other words, we have no right to privacy in the way we smell when we are out in public. And police who detect these odors are not conducting searches. Passive alcohol sensors have been used for two decades and no court has held [that] their use violates the Constitution.

Some people argue that if it is not illegal it is still unfair to use a sensor without notifying drivers in advance. It does make good sense to alert the public that sensors are being used; if people know police have effective ways of identifying the presence of alcohol, drivers with high BACs may be deterred from driving. But police are not required to tell citizens what is being done to enforce the law. For example, courts do not require police at sobriety checkpoints to tell drivers about the traditional ways officers look for signs of high BACs, such as listening for slurred speech, or looking for a lack of coordination when drivers look for their licenses and vehicle registrations.

Police using traditional techniques to identify high-BAC drivers are missing too many of them. The passive alcohol sensor is a reliable and legal tool that should become standard in police efforts to identify and investigate drivers with high BACs.

12

Police Use of Passive Alcohol Sensors Erodes Civil Liberties

Eric Peters

Eric Peters is a journalist based in Washington, D.C., who frequently writes about the impact of automotive regulations on consumers.

The PAS (passive alcohol sensor) III Sniffer is a new device that police departments are using to detect drunk drivers. The Sniffer is built into a flashlight and can estimate a driver's blood-alcohol content by sampling exhaled breath as the driver responds to an officer's questions during a routine traffic stop. Supporters of PAS devices argue that they give police an effective tool to catch dangerous drunks who might otherwise pass undetected through sobriety checkpoints. But these devices subject drivers to an unreasonable search by taking breath samples without the driver's knowledge or consent. "Sniffing" all drivers stopped by police officers before signs of intoxication are exhibited represents an affront to the Constitution, reversing the legal standard that holds people innocent until proven guilty.

Big Brother has a new technological toy in his toolbox—a "flashlight" that is actually a kind of breath analyzer that can be used to sample your exhalations for signs of alcohol—without you ever knowing you're being tested.

Device erodes civil liberties

The PAS (passive alcohol sensor) III Sniffer is able to estimate a person's blood-alcohol content based on just four seconds of conversation—such as when a cop asks you for your license and registration during a routine traffic stop. A pump inside the flashlight's body draws in a sample of the subject's exhaled breath through a fuel cell, which generates a voltage response about the presence of alcohol vapor; a color display then flashes

Excerpted from Eric Peters, "Sniffer Promises a Secret Way to Deflate People's Liberties," *The Detroit News*, September 7, 2000. Copyright © 2000, *The Detroit News*, a Gannet Newspaper. Reprinted with permission from *The Detroit News*.

red for a liquored-up driver, green for teetotaler.

Police love the idea. It is in use in West Lafayette, Indiana, and some other Midwestern locations, but not Michigan yet. Police officers see the device as a more efficient way to corral impaired drivers who might otherwise slip the gantlet. But people who are concerned about their rapidly eroding civil liberties should be concerned.

Unlike the familiar Breathalyzer, which requires a subject to blow into a device that gives a readout of blood-alcohol levels—or even the field sobriety test, where an officer asks a suspected drunk driver to perform simple physical tests that evaluate impairment—the PAS III Sniffer does its work without your knowledge or consent.

"For many years, your privacy rights and the right of police to investigate was kept in balance by the available technology," says Kent Willis of the American Civil Liberties Union. "That balance has been destroyed."

An assumption of guilt

The Sniffer dispenses with the cumbersome (to police) Fourth Amendment, which prohibits unreasonable searches and seizures. While Sniffer supporters may argue that the device will help apprehend dangerous drunks, it lets them evade the issue of whether this noble goal is worth subjecting everyone to a "search" without their consent or knowledge—and before they have done a single thing to suggest they've been drinking.

John W. Whitehead of the conservative Rutherford Institute, a Washington think tank, told the *Washington Post* that the Sniffer is an egregious affront to the Fourth Amendment. "To catch a possible drunk driver, do we throw the Constitution in the garbage can? I say no." The Sniffer, he said, "assumes you're guilty. It reverses the standard of proof. Why are they sniffing you if they don't think you're guilty? Next, they're going to be sniffing for cigarettes."

> *The Sniffer dispenses with the cumbersome (to police) Fourth Amendment, which prohibits unreasonable searches and seizures.*

Police in my hometown area of Fairfax County, Virginia, are among the most fervent advocates of the $600 Sniffers. Officers have used them at both sobriety checkpoints as well as during regular patrols. "So far they've worked really well," says Lt. Dennis O'Neill.

Certainly. As would body cavity searches of all airline passengers. Or random frisks on the street. The chilling refrain, "Your papers, please" may not have died out with the Gestapo or Soviet Russia's NKVD [secret police]. If such "tools" as the Sniffer—not to mention asset forfeiture laws and the related apocrypha of law-enforcement overkill—are allowed to stand, then we have accepted, at least in principle, the foundation of a future total state that may come to resemble something potentially far worse than the tyrannies of the past.

Technology is making a level of surveillance possible that could not have been imagined by Nazi Minister of Propaganda Joseph Goebbels or

Soviet secret police chief Lavrenty Beria.

PAS Systems of Fredericksburg, Virginia, has already sold several thousand Sniffers to police departments around the country—including the federal Park Police.

Less effort for police, less privacy for the public

Naturally, the insurance industry and Mothers Against Drunk Driving (MADD) organization are falling over themselves to embrace this ugly business. "People who were driving drunk were able to brace themselves up and have a 50-50 chance of getting through a checkpoint," says Tim Hoyt of Nationwide Insurance. "That's what got us interested" in the Sniffer technology. Mike Green of MADD says the Sniffer "saves the police a lot of effort" in trying to figure out if someone has been drinking.

This is all quite true but beside the point. It would also "save the police a lot of effort" if they could just randomly stop and frisk people, too—or bust down their doors and search their homes without a warrant. Surely, a great many drug dealers, child pornographers and so on could be apprehended this way. But we would be living in a police state, then, wouldn't we?

To date, the use of the Sniffer has not been challenged in court. According to some legal experts, the device will probably survive any future legal challenge, too—because the Sniffer only samples the air after it has left the driver's body. This smacks of the amoral legalistic parsing that has also justified asset forfeiture laws, such as those that enable the government to seize boats and homes, without the owner having been found guilty—and often not even charged—with any crime.

Legalisms notwithstanding, people have cause to be worried.

13

All Drunk Driving Offenders Should Lose Their Cars

Rudolph Giuliani

Rudolph Giuliani is the mayor of New York City.

In response to the declining but still unacceptable number of alcohol-related traffic fatalities occurring in New York City and its surrounding metropolitan area, the New York City Police Department initiated the policy of confiscating the cars of those arrested for driving while intoxicated (DWI) in February 1999. This policy not only takes lethal weapons off the road, it also works as a highly effective deterrent against potential drunk drivers, making them think long and hard about risking the loss of their motor vehicle if stopped by the police. The policy is intended to stop first-time offenders, who cause the majority of DWI fatalities nationwide, in addition to the chronic drunk drivers who routinely put the lives of others at risk.

Drunk driving is one of our most tragic social problems. Thousands of families every year lose loved ones because people fail to exercise the basic responsibility to abstain from drinking when they are going to drive an automobile. Every one of those deaths is preventable—but for years, despite extensive public education campaigns, the message hasn't gotten across clearly enough.

Counting the fatalities

In the United States in 1998, there were 41,471 traffic fatalities. Of those, nearly 16,000—or over 38 percent—were alcohol-related. That's a slight decline from 1997, but still, clearly, a crime of major proportions. In New York State, we suffered 1,498 traffic fatalities on our roads in 1998, and 24 percent of that total, or 365—an average of one every day—were alcohol-related. That also represents a reduction—a 22 percent decline from the 1997 New York State total, in fact—and is a sign that we are moving in the right direction.

Education and enforcement make the difference

What accounts for our progress? In New York City, it's largely the result of effective law enforcement efforts combined with intense and unrelenting public education. That approach has made a difference. In 1997, we had 51 Driving While Intoxicated (DWI) fatalities citywide. A year later, that number had dropped to 33. But we need to go further because far too many lives are still taken at the hands of drunk drivers.

Confiscating cars saves lives

That's why in February of 1999 the New York City Police Department launched an aggressive new initiative to confiscate the cars of those arrested for Driving While Intoxicated.

The policy saves lives in two ways. First, it takes lethal weapons off the road—and we can quantify exactly how many. Since the start of the program, we've seized more than 1,200 vehicles.

Too many lives are still taken at the hands of drunk drivers.

And then there's an effect that we cannot as easily quantify: deterrence. We wanted to do everything we possibly could to make people think a second, third, fourth, or fifth time—whatever it would take to make them stop before getting behind the wheel of a car. Because it's never worth it to drive while intoxicated. It's never harmless. It's never excusable. It always a grave, grave error and a crime.

The signs are that our approach is working. Since the implementation of the initiative, the number of DWI crashes in New York City has dropped more than 17 percent compared to the same time period last year, the number of DWI fatalities has declined by 18 percent, and the number of people we have to arrest for DWI has fallen by 24 percent.

Cracking down on first-time offenders

This is a policy that, properly enforced, has the potential to be a breakthrough in the fight against drunk driving. In fact, it's already being emulated across our state and around the country. Some people say, why do you confiscate the vehicles of first-time offenders? Why don't you wait until they are caught driving drunk a second time?

Those who understand this crime, however, know that the majority of DWI fatalities nationwide—the vast majority, in fact—are caused by first-time offenders. Our local statistic show the same trend. There have been 22 DWI fatalities in New York since February 22, when our vehicle-seizure program began. Thirteen of those fatalities have been the drunk drivers themselves. Of the remaining nine—the nine drunk drivers who we have arrested for taking the lives of innocent human beings—each and every one was a first-time offender.

Seizing deadly weapons

The point is to stop the first-time offenders, as well as to catch the chronic drunk drivers who put the lives of others at risk on a regular basis. We don't care whose deadly weapon we're taking off the road. The point is to save lives.

We will continue to do just that. And we'll realize one other fundamentally important point: government cannot win the fight if it has to go alone. The only way to make profound long-term progress is to change people's minds one at a time. To do this, we will always depend upon families and friends to continue teaching one another the critical importance of understanding their responsibilities to other human beings each and every time they get behind the wheel.

14

Only Repeat Drunk Driving Offenders Should Lose Their Cars

Paul Kursky

Paul Kursky is a staff writer for Louis *magazine, a publication of Brandeis University.*

In February 1999, New York City Mayor Rudolph Giuliani instituted the policy of using criminal forfeiture laws to confiscate the cars of motorists convicted of drunk driving. Although twenty-three states have laws that allow for the confiscation or impoundment of cars as a penalty for drunk driving, New York City is unique in that its confiscation policy applies to first-time offenders. To get their cars returned, those accused of drunk driving are subject to both a criminal and civil trial. Because civil trials have lower standards for guilt, defendants could conceivably be found not guilty of drunk driving in a criminal trial yet still lose their cars if found liable in civil court. Taking cars away from the criminally innocent is unjust, and this extreme policy should be limited to repeat drunk driving offenders, whose behavior poses the biggest threat to road safety.

Just in case anyone out there is still not wary of the penalties for driving drunk, New York City has decided to add yet another weapon to its arsenal in the fight against idiots who think it's OK to slam back a few and then go out for a spin. In late February 1999, New York City mayor Rudolph Giuliani announced that city police would begin seizing the cars of anyone caught driving with a blood alcohol content (BAC) higher than .1 percent.

New York City's tough policy

This is not a particularly new concept in law enforcement. In fact, according to CNN.com, 23 states in the US have laws on the books that al-

---

low for the confiscation or impoundment of cars as a penalty for drunk driving. These laws, however, generally apply to repeat offenders; New York City's policy is not reserved only for the continually stupid, because first-time offenders are subject to this penalty as well. In addition, only New York City has used its already existing laws of criminal forfeiture to actually take possession of such vehicles. (These are the types of statutes that allow the government to seize the belongings of drug dealers and other such "model" citizens.)

This time the boys in blue mean business. Hopefully, this will help lower the amount of deaths from drunk driving incidents in the city, which in 1998 totaled 31. All in all, 6,000 people were arrested in 1998 in New York City for driving with BACs that were too high.

Seizing cars from innocent drivers

There is a second facet to New York City's new policy, as articulated by [Brandeis University] Professor Ed Koch (the scariest part about this element of Giuliani's law is that I agree with the former mayor). As everyone who comes into contact with [former New York City] Mayor Koch knows, he and Mayor Giuliani aren't the best of pals. In his class here at Brandeis a few weeks ago, he discussed the current mayor's policy. Koch doesn't think very highly of the mayor's Zero-Tolerance Drinking and Driving Initiative, and here's why: innocent people can have their cars taken away, too.

---

23 states in the US have laws on the books that allow for the confiscation or impoundment of cars as a penalty for drunk driving.

As hard as that is to believe, it is true. After having their cars confiscated, offenders are sent to trial in criminal court, like they would be in any other city. However, in New York City, a civil trial is conducted concurrently with the criminal trial. Even if the defendant is found not guilty in criminal court, his car can still be kept and auctioned off if he is found liable in civil court. The problem with this is the criteria for guilt in civil cases are much less than those in criminal cases. This means that even if it turns out your BAC *wasn't* that high, you could still lose your car forever.

Only repeat offenders should lose their cars

To me, seizing the cars of convicted drunk drivers is not the worst idea in the world. It truly disgusts me that there are people out there who think it's perfectly safe to go driving after they've been sippin' "Grandpa's cough medicine." Drunk driving is one of the most selfish acts a person could ever hope to commit. Not only are the morons who choose to do this endangering themselves, they're putting in jeopardy the lives of any other person who decides to go near a road that night as well. I think the policy would be better suited if it pertained to repeat offenders only. After all, it's these people who are the real menace to the roads. While you shouldn't be drinking and driving to begin with, you shouldn't be driving period if you're going to drive drunk over and over again. These people continue to get off with comparative slaps on the wrists. Did we give Ted Kaczynski back his bomb-making materials? Did we hand back Sammy "the Bull" Gravano his Beretta and say, "Keep up the good work?" No. So why have we let drunk drivers keep their cars?

The policy would be better suited if it pertained to repeat offenders only.

I am glad that no other state has a law like this one. Not because I drive drunk in any of those forty-nine, but because the law is extreme. Both innocent drivers and first-time offenders do not deserve to have their cars seized—their livelihoods and their means of connection to everything around them should not be taken away from them. The law can be tough while being a tool for reform, but it should be tough only to a point; Giuliani has gone beyond that point. Taking cars away from criminally innocent people is insane.

This time Herr Rudy has gone too far. People who are found not guilty should be treated like they are not guilty. This is excessive. This is repressive. This is wrong.

15

Drunk Driving Should Be Legalized

Llewellyn H. Rockwell Jr.

Llewellyn H. Rockwell Jr. is president of the Ludwig von Mises Institute, a conservative research and educational center.

In ordering states to enforce tougher drunk driving standards by making it a crime to drive with a blood-alcohol concentration of .08 percent or higher, government has been permitted to criminalize the content of drivers' blood instead of their actions. The assumption that a driver who has been drinking automatically presents a danger to society even when no harm has been caused is a blatant violation of civil liberties. Government should not be concerned with the probability and propensity of a drinking driver to cause an accident; rather, laws should deal only with actions that damage person or property. Until they actually commit a crime, drunk drivers should be liberated from the force of the law.

[Former President Bill] Clinton signed a bill passed by Congress [in October 2000] that orders the states to adopt new, more onerous drunk-driving standards or face a loss of highway funds. That's right: the old highway extortion trick. Sure enough, states are already working to pass new, tighter laws against driving under the influence (DUI), responding as expected to the fed's ransom note.

Criminalizing alcohol consumption

Now the feds declare that a blood-alcohol level of 0.08 percent and above is criminal and must be severely punished. The National Restaurant Association is exactly right that this is absurdly low. The overwhelming majority of accidents related to drunk driving involve repeat offenders with blood-alcohol levels twice that high. If a standard of 0.1 doesn't deter them, then a lower one won't either.

But there's a more fundamental point. What precisely is being criminalized? Not bad driving. Not destruction of property. Not the taking of

Reprinted from "Legalize Drunk Driving," by Llewellyn H. Rockwell Jr., WorldNetDaily.com, November 2, 2000. Reprinted with permission.

human life or reckless endangerment. The crime is having the wrong substance in your blood. Yet it is possible, in fact, to have this substance in your blood, even while driving, and not commit anything like what has been traditionally called a crime.

What have we done by permitting government to criminalize the content of our blood instead of actions themselves? We have given it power to make the application of the law arbitrary, capricious and contingent on the judgment of cops and cop technicians. Indeed, without the government's Breathalyzer, there is no way to tell for sure if we are breaking the law.

Sure, we can do informal calculations in our head, based on our weight and the amount of alcohol we have had over some period of time. But at best these will be estimates. We have to wait for the government to administer a test to tell us whether or not we are criminals. That's not the way law is supposed to work. Indeed, this is a form of tyranny.

Government and probabilities

Now, the immediate response goes this way: drunk driving has to be illegal because the probability of causing an accident rises dramatically when you drink. The answer is just as simple: government in a free society should not deal in probabilities. The law should deal in actions and actions alone, and only insofar as they damage person or property. Probabilities are something for insurance companies to assess on a competitive and voluntary basis.

This is why the campaign against racial profiling has intuitive plausibility to many people: surely a person shouldn't be hounded solely because some demographic groups have higher crime rates than others. Government should be preventing and punishing crimes themselves, not probabilities and propensities. Neither, then, should we have driver profiling, which assumes that, just because a person has quaffed a few, he is automatically a danger.

It is possible . . . to have [alcohol] in your blood, even while driving, and not commit anything like what has been traditionally called a crime.

In fact, driver profiling is worse than racial profiling, because the latter only implies that the police are more watchful, not that they criminalize race itself. Despite the propaganda, what's being criminalized in the case of drunk driving is *not* the probability that a person driving will get into an accident but the *fact* of the blood-alcohol content itself. A drunk driver is humiliated and destroyed even when he hasn't done any harm.

Of course, enforcement is a serious problem. A sizeable number of people leaving a bar or a restaurant would probably qualify as DUI. But there is no way for the police to know unless they are tipped off by a swerving car or reckless driving in general. But the question becomes: why not ticket the swerving or recklessness and leave the alcohol out of it? Why indeed.

To underscore the fact that it is some level of drinking that is being criminalized, government sets up these outrageous, civil-liberties-violating barricades that stop people to check their blood—even when they have done nothing at all. This is a gross attack on liberty that implies that the government has and should have total control over us, extending even to the testing of intimate biological facts. But somehow we put up with it because we have conceded the first assumption that government ought to punish us for the content of our blood and not just our actions.

There are many factors that cause a person to drive poorly. You may have sore muscles after a weight-lifting session and have slow reactions. You could be sleepy. You could be in a bad mood, or angry after a fight with your spouse. Should the government be allowed to administer anger tests, tiredness tests, or soreness tests? That is the very next step, and don't be surprised when Congress starts to examine this question.

Already, there's a move on to prohibit cell phone use while driving. Such an absurdity follows from the idea that government should make judgments about what we are allegedly likely to do.

Whether sober or drunk, accidents happen

What's more, some people drive *more* safely after a few drinks, precisely because they know their reaction time has been slowed and they must pay more attention to safety. We all know drunks who have an amazing ability to drive perfectly after being liquored up. They should be liberated from the force of the law and only punished if they actually do something wrong.

Government should be preventing and punishing crimes themselves, not probabilities and propensities.

We need to put a stop to this whole trend now. Drunk driving should be legalized. And please don't write me to say:

I am offended by your insensitivity because my mother was killed by a drunk driver.

Any person responsible for killing someone else is guilty of manslaughter or murder and should be punished accordingly. But it is perverse to punish a murderer not because of his crime but because of some biological consideration, e.g., he has red hair.

Bank robbers may tend to wear masks, but the crime they commit has nothing to do with the mask. In the same way, drunk drivers cause accidents, but so do sober drivers, and many drunk drivers cause no accidents at all. The law should focus on violations of person and property, not scientific oddities like blood content.

There's a final point against Clinton's drunk-driving bill. It is a violation of states' rights. Not only is there no warrant in the Constitution for the federal government to legislate blood-alcohol content—the 10th Amendment should prevent it from doing so. The question of drunk driving should first be returned to the states, and then each state should liberate drunk drivers from the force of the law.

Organizations to Contact

The editors have compiled the following list of organizations concerned with the issues presented in this book. Descriptions are derived from materials provided by the organizations. All have publications or information available for interested readers. The list was compiled on the date of publication of the present volume; names, addresses, phone and fax numbers, and e-mail/Internet addresses may change. Be aware that many organizations take several weeks or longer to respond to inquiries, so allow as much time as possible.

Against Drunk Driving (ADD)
PO Box 397, Station A, Brampton, ON L6V 2L3 Canada
(905) 793-4233 • fax: (905) 793-7035
e-mail: add@netcom.ca • website: www.add.ca

Founded in 1983, ADD is a grassroots organization that strives to reduce death and injury caused by impaired drivers through educating the public about the dangers of drunk driving. The organization's Victims Self-Help program provides counseling for people who have lost loved ones in drunk driving accidents. ADD also holds presentations for alcohol-impaired drivers in correctional facilities as part of a six-week rehabilitation program called GUARD (Greater Understanding on Alcohol Related Driving). ADD's group for young adults, Teen-ADD, holds conferences, workshops, and presentations to raise awareness about the problem of teen drunk driving. ADD publishes the quarterly newsletter *ADDvisor*, which is also available on its website.

American Beverage Institute (ABI)
1775 Pennsylvania Ave. NW, Suite 1200, Washington, DC 20006
(800) 843-8877
e-mail: abi@abionline.org • website: www.abionline.org

ABI is an association of restaurant operators that serve alcohol. The institute believes that anti-alcohol activists have gone too far in trying to restrict the consumption of adult beverages. Through education and research efforts, ABI is working to convince state governments that .08 percent blood-alcohol concentration (BAC) limits are ineffective. It publishes the *ABI Newsletter* along with numerous reports on the impact of BAC laws.

Boaters Against Drunk Driving (BADD)
141-B Landmark St., Deltona, FL 32725-8027
(407) 574-7153
e-mail: SafeBoating@badd.org • website: www.badd.org

BADD is dedicated to promoting safe, sober, and responsible boating throughout the United States and Canada. Through its Judicial Watch, the organization monitors cases of individuals charged with boating under the influence of alcohol (BUI); BADD publishes the progress of these cases to demonstrate to the boating community and the general public that state boating officials, legislators, prosecutors, and courts all consider BUI a very serious crime. As a memorial to the victims of BUI tragedies, BADD has implemented a project

87

called Lighthouse of Law. BADD's website also includes statistics, charts, and articles concerning the dangers of boating under the influence of alcohol.

Center for Substance Abuse Prevention (CSAP)
National Clearinghouse for Alcohol and Drug Information (NCADI)
PO Box 2345, Rockville, MD 20847-2345
(800) 729-6686 • fax: (301) 468-6433
e-mail: info@health.org • website: www.health.org

The CSAP leads U.S. government efforts to prevent alcoholism and other substance abuse problems among Americans. Through the NCADI, the center provides the public with a wide variety of information concerning alcohol abuse, including the problem of drunk driving. Its publications include the bimonthly *Prevention Pipeline*, the report "Impaired Driving Among Youth: Trends and Tools for Prevention," brochures, pamphlets, videotapes, and posters. Publications in Spanish are also available.

Century Council
1310 G St. NW, Suite 600, Washington, DC 20005
(202) 637-0077 • fax: (202) 637-0079
e-mail: jonesb@centurycouncil.org • website: www.centurycouncil.org

Funded by America's leading distillers, the Century Council is a not-for-profit, national organization committed to fighting underage drinking and reducing alcohol-related crashes. The council promotes legislative efforts to pass tough drunk driving laws and works with the alcohol industry to help servers and sellers prevent drunk driving. Its interactive CD-ROM, *Alcohol 101*, provides "virtual" scenarios to help students make sensible, fact-based decisions about drinking.

Distilled Spirits Council of the United States (DISCUS)
1250 Eye St. NW, Suite 400, Washington, DC 20005
(202) 628-3544
website: www.discus.health.org

The Distilled Spirits Council of the United States is the national trade association representing producers and marketers of distilled spirits in the United States. It seeks to ensure the responsible use of distilled spirits by adult consumers and to curb alcohol abuse and underage drinking. DISCUS publishes fact sheets, the periodic newsletter *News Release*, and several pamphlets, including *The Drunk Driving Prevention Act*.

Entertainment Industries Council (EIC)
1760 Reston Pkwy., Suite 415, Reston, VA 20190-3330
(703) 481-1414 • fax: (703) 481-1418
e-mail: eic@eiconline.org • website: www.eiconline.org

The EIC works to educate the entertainment industry and audiences about major public health and social issues. Its members strive to effect social change by providing educational materials, research, and training to the entertainment industry. The EIC publishes several fact sheets concerning alcohol abuse and alcohol-impaired driving.

Mothers Against Drunk Driving (MADD)
PO Box 541688, Dallas, TX 75354-1688
(214) 744-6233 • fax: (214) 869-2209
e-mail: info@madd.org • website: www.madd.org

A nationwide grassroots organization, MADD provides support services to victims of drunk driving and attempts to influence policy makers by lobbying for changes in legislation on local, state, and national levels. MADD's public education efforts include its "Rating the States" report, which draws attention to the status of state and federal efforts against drunk driving. MADD publishes the semiannual *Driven* magazine and numerous pamphlets and brochures, including *Someone You Know Drinks and Drives, Financial Recovery After a Drunk Driving Crash,* and *Drunk Driving: An Unacknowledged Form of Child Endangerment.*

National Commission Against Drunk Driving (NCADD)
1900 L St. NW, Suite 705, Washington, DC 20036
(202) 452-6004 • fax: (202) 223-7012
e-mail: ncadd@trafficsafety.org • website: www.ncadd.com

NCADD comprises public and private sector leaders who are dedicated to minimizing the human and economic losses resulting from motor vehicle crashes by making impaired driving a socially unacceptable act. Working with private sector groups and federal, state, and local officials, NCADD develops strategies to target the three most intractable groups of drunk drivers: underage drinkers, young adults, and chronic drunk drivers. The commission's publications include research abstracts, traffic safety facts, the reports "The Dummy's Guide to Youth Alcohol Programs" and "Chronic Drunk Drivers: Resources Available to Keep Them Off the Road," and a guide for parent/teen discussion, "Yes, You May Use the Car, but FIRST . . .".

National Highway Traffic Safety Administration (NHTSA)
Impaired Driving Division
400 Seventh St. SW, Washington, DC 20590
(202) 366-2683 ext. 2728
website: www.nhtsa.dot.gov/people/injury/alcohol

The NHTSA allocates funds for states to demonstrate the effectiveness of visible enforcement initiatives against drunk driving. The mission of its Impaired Driving Division is to save lives, prevent injuries, and reduce traffic-related health care and economic costs resulting from impaired driving. The organization's publications concerning impaired driving include the pamphlet *Get the Keys* and the manual *Strategies for Success: Combating Juvenile DUI,* which provides tools to help develop a comprehensive criminal justice system response to underage drunk driving.

Students Against Destructive Decisions (SADD)
PO Box 800, Marlboro, MA 01752
(508) 481-3568 • fax: (508) 481-5759
website: www.saddonline.com

Formerly called Students Against Drunk Driving, SADD is a school-based organization dedicated to addressing the issues of underage drinking, impaired driving, drug use, and other destructive decisions that harm young people. SADD seeks to provide students with prevention and intervention tools that build the confidence needed to make healthy choices and behavioral changes. These tools include "never again" campaigns in honor of students killed in drunk driving accidents, candlelight vigils, impact scenarios, and student surveys on teens' attitudes and concerns about drinking and driving. SADD also holds conferences and publishes a triannual newsletter.

Bibliography

Books

Nathan Aaseng — *Teens and Drunk Driving.* San Diego: Lucent Books, 2000.

Deborah Chrisfield — *Drinking and Driving.* Mankato, MN: Crestwood House, 1995.

Robyn L. Cohen — *Drunk Driving.* Washington, DC: U.S. Department of Justice, 1992.

Denis Foley, ed. — *Stop DWI: Successful Community Responses to Drunk Driving.* Lexington, MA: Lexington Books, 1986.

Sandy Golden — *How to Save Lives and Reduce Injuries: A Citizen Activist Guide to Effectively Fight Drunk Driving.* Washington, DC: U.S. Department of Transportation, 1983.

James B. Jacobs — *Drunk Driving, an American Dilemma.* Chicago: University of Chicago Press, 1989.

Jean McBee Knox — *Drinking, Driving, and Drugs.* New York: Chelsea House, 1998.

Laura M. Maruschak — *DWI Offenders Under Correctional Supervision.* Washington, DC: U.S. Department of Justice, 1999.

National Highway Traffic Safety Administration — *State of Knowledge of Alcohol-Impaired Driving: Research on Repeat DWI Offenders.* Washington, DC: U.S. Department of Transportation, 2000.

Gerald D. Robin — *Waging the Battle Against Drunk Driving.* Westport, CT: Greenwood, 1991.

H.L. Ross — *Confronting Drunk Driving: Social Policy for Saving Lives.* New Haven, CT: Yale University Press, 1994.

Elsie R. Shore and Joseph R. Ferrari, eds. — *Preventing Drunk Driving.* Binghamton, NY: Haworth, 1998.

Frank A. Sloan, ed. — *Drinkers, Drivers, and Bartenders: Balancing Private and Public Accountability.* Chicago: University of Chicago Press, 2000.

Periodicals

Alcoholism and Drug Abuse Weekly — "More States Back .08 Legislation," April 9, 2001.

Brandy Anderson — "Congress Passes National .08 BAC Law," *Driven,* Fall 2000.

Patrick Bedard — "The Deadly Drivers Are Deadly Drunk," *Car & Driver,* September 1998.

Ira Berkow	"Alcohol Abuse Ends Two Lives and Wrecks Another," *New York Times,* April 25, 1999.
Keith Bradsher	"Fatalities from Drunken Driving Drop, but Total Traffic Deaths Hold Steady," *New York Times,* August 25, 1998.
David Byrd	"Last Call for Alcohol?" *National Journal,* December 18, 1999.
Doc Carney	"Am I Free to Go?" *Patriot News Online,* Patriotnews.com, December 8, 2000.
Consumers' Research Magazine	"How Effective Are '.08' Drunk-Driving Laws?" August 1999.
Drivers.com	"The Case for .08 BAC: Science vs. Myth," April 4, 1999.
Drivers.com	"Merits of a .08 BAC Per Se Law for Adult Drivers," September 9, 1999.
Alan Finder	"Drive Drunk, Lose the Car? Principle Faces a Test," *New York Times,* February 24, 1999.
Melanie Franklin	"My Daughter Was a Drunk Driver," *Good Housekeeping,* August 1998.
David Frum	"When Drunk Driving Was Cool," *Wall Street Journal,* November 6, 2000.
Mary P. Gallagher	"Civil Libertarians Wince at New Device That 'Shines Light' on Drunken Drivers," *New Jersey Law Journal,* August 21, 2000.
Jim Holt	"A MADD Law," *Wall Street Journal,* March 5, 1998.
Paul Kersey	"Governing While Intoxicated by Good Intentions," FreeCitizen.com, April 21, 1999.
Kathy Koch	"Drunken Driving," *CQ Researcher,* October 6, 2000.
Lancet	"Driving Under the Influence," December 12, 1998.
Irvin Molotsky	"U.S. Cites Drop in Arrests for Drunken Driving," *New York Times,* June 17, 1999.
Mark Murray	"Unbottling the .08 Percent Solution," *National Journal,* November 4, 2000.
Eric Nagourney	"A Sobering Effect on Teenagers," *New York Times,* May 8, 2001.
New York Times	"Support for New Alcohol Standard," April 10, 2001.
Brian Pace	"Driving Safely by Avoiding Alcohol," *Journal of the American Medical Association,* May 3, 2000.
Eric Peters	"MADD House," *National Review,* September 28, 1998.
Jane Prendergast	"Mahoney Case Puts Focus on DUI Law," *Cincinnati Enquirer,* September 2, 1999.
Elaine Rivera	"License to Drink," *Time,* July 31, 2000.

Stephen Simon   "Medical Staff Reporting of Alcohol Levels Should Be
                     Mandatory," *Washington Post,* December 13, 1999.

Carl A. Soderstrom   "Testing Injured Drivers for Blood Alcohol Content Is
                     Valuable," *Washington Post,* December 13, 1999.

Jacob Sullum   "Drink and Drive, Lose Your Car," *Conservative Chronicle,*
                     April 12, 1999.

Robert B. Voas   "Higher-Risk Driver Crackdown," *Driven,* Spring 1999.

Matthew L. Wald   "States, Getting Tougher on Drunken Drivers, Seize
                     Cars," *New York Times,* July 19, 1998.

Rob Waldron   "Students Are Dying; Colleges Can Do More," *Newsweek,*
                     October 30, 2000.

Wall Street Journal "B.A.D.D.," February 25, 1999.

Jason K. Wells   "Drinking Drivers Missed at Sobriety Checkpoints," *Journal of Studies on Alcohol,* September 1997.

Index